SACRAMENTO PUBLIC LIBRARY

SAC

SA , CA 95814

1/2009

Grammar
for the Soul

Grammar
for the Soul

*Using Language
for Personal Change*

LAWRENCE A. WEINSTEIN

QUEST

BOOKS

Theosophical Publishing House
Wheaton, Illinois • Chennai, India

Copyright © 2008 by Lawrence A. Weinstein

First Quest edition 2008

All rights reserved. No part of this book may be reproduced in any manner without written permission except for quotations embedded in critical articles or reviews. For additional information write to

Quest Books
Theosophical Publishing House
P.O. Box 270
Wheaton, IL 60189-0270

www.questbooks.net

Cover image: © ImageZoo/Images.com
Cover design, book design, and typesetting by Dan Doolin

Library of Congress Cataloging-in-Publication Data

Weinstein, Larry.
Grammar for the soul: using language for personal change / Lawrence A. Weinstein.—1st Quest ed.
    p.   cm.
Includes bibliographical references and index.
ISBN 978-0-8356-0865-7
1. English language—Miscellanea.   2. English language—Grammar.   I. Title.
PE1095.W35 2008
425—dc22   2007044937

5   4   3   2   1   *   08   09   10   11   12

Printed in the United States of America

To Diane

*To know how near or
far each soul is from its goal,
the indicator is speech.*

—NACHMAN OF BRATZLAV

Editorial Note

Note numbers do not appear in the text. All textual references are listed in the sources section at the end of the book.

Contents

Introduction   1

**Bootstrap Grammar—Taking
   Life in Hand**   7

GETTING NOTICED   9
Colons

ENERGY   13
Transitive Verbs in the Active Voice

WHEREWITHAL   18
Prepositions

DOING WHAT WORKS   20
Anomalous Commas and Beyond

LACK OF TIME   25
The Imperative

Grammar for Creative Passivity   29

GETTING OUT OF ONE'S
      OWN WAY   32
Passive Voice

THE LATENT REPERTOIRE   36
Triple-Spacing

HYBRID   40
Blessing

Grammar for Belonging   43

TOUCH   46
Many Elements

COMMUNICATION   52
Commas, Quotation Marks, Modifiers,
Pronouns

BONDING   57
Ellipses

BEING CORRECT   61
Apostrophes

COMPROMISE   65
"They"—Made Singular

TRUST   71
Exclamation Marks, Italics, Intensifiers

GENEROSITY   75
Semicolons, Cumulative Sentences

FRIENDS IN THE GRAVEYARD   80
Present Tense

Grammar for Freedom   85

MODELING I-STATEMENTS   88

USING E-PRIME   91

SHIFTING INTO PAST TENSE   95

OUR LINGUISTIC LIMITS   98

Grammar to Restore the Ego 101

FULCRUM 103
"But"

GRAMMAR, THING OF BEAUTY 105
Sentence Length and Repetition,
among Other Things

Grammar for Mindfulness 111

SPEAKING WITHOUT FEIGNING CERTAINTY: PART I 115
Avoiding the Third-Person Omniscient

SPEAKING WITHOUT FEIGNING CERTAINTY: PART II 118
Emily Dickinson's Dashes

CHECKING PREOCCUPATION 121
Future Tense and Adverbial Provisos

A DIGRESSION ON THE SPIRITUAL VALUE OF DICTIONARIES 125

TOLERATING AMBIGUITY 129
"And"

CODA 133

ACKNOWLEDGMENTS 135

SOURCES 139

INDEX 150

Introduction

*The limits of my language mean
the limits of my world.*
—LUDWIG WITTGENSTEIN

Grammar? In most people's minds, the closest synonym for "grammar" is "chore." It's about as inspiring a thought as "dust cloth." It certainly seems to have no place in a discussion of ways to realize one's potential as a whole person.

All the same, I wish to suggest that our list of activities capable of hastening personal growth be expanded beyond yoga, meditation, and the martial arts to include the wise use of syntax and punctuation.

During my first twenty years as a teacher of writing at the college level, I would not have dreamed of suggesting this idea. Like my colleagues, I viewed grammar's importance strictly in terms of communication: only by following its rules can we *Homo sapiens* make our thoughts clear to one another. A randomly ordered, unmarked string of words such as "you rake hand me that would" is gibberish, whereas the correctly sequenced, punctuated sentence "Would you hand me that rake?" gets the job done. That was grammar's great contribution to us—but its *only* contribution, insofar as I could tell.

If, during those first twenty years in the classroom, I saw a connection between grammar and mental health, it was a negative one: a sizeable fraction of my students at both Harvard University and Bentley College had been verbally traumatized in the name of grammar. Their high school teachers had red-marked their papers so heavily for split infinitives, tense shifts, pronoun reference problems, run-ons, fragments, and the like that now they feared committing words to paper at all. They approached blank sheets of paper as they might a minefield. I actually once wrote an essay on those students' behalf entitled "Grammar, What Big Teeth You Have."

I did not begin to think about how attention to grammar can *enhance* morale until I read some articles by linguist Benjamin Lee Whorf. According to him, any language—English or Hopi or Chinese—does more than enable its speakers to make their thinking clear to each other: it somewhat molds their thinking. By making it easier to express certain thoughts than others (and which thoughts those are, he says, differs from language to language), *a language helps determine what one thinks and feels in the first place.* In English, for example, we have tenses that separate the present from the past— that put the past behind us, in effect, implying it will never come again—and most of us who *think* in English therefore try not to "waste" time; we move in a hurry. By comparison, the Hopi Indians Whorf studied— whose management of tense implied that "everything that ever happened still is"—had less incentive to live fast and therefore led more measured lives. A language,

Whorf believed, can contribute either to neuroses (his term) or to more expansive, adaptive ways of thinking and being.

When I encountered Whorf, I knew little about differences between whole national grammars but a fair amount about differences between the grammar of one English speaker and the grammar of another. Each of my students represented a distinct grammatical profile *within* English. One never used a question mark—or a hedging phrase or clause—but would use italics and adverbial intensifiers ("without doubt," "very," "extremely," etc.) freely. Another stood out for inserting the occasional parenthesis or dash as a conversational touch. A third wrote sentences so long that they created the impression she couldn't bear to part with them, and a fourth wrote only sentences of twenty-two words or less, each built along the simplest of lines from subject to predicate to object. In the course of reading Whorf, I began to wonder if his central insight applied to all these *private* languages as well as national ones. Could these linguistic differences be linked to different ways of thinking and living? If so, that seemed worth knowing, since making the right changes in one's grammar might then be expected to improve one's life, to some degree.

Deciding to test my thesis on the speaker with whom I had the most influence, I resolved to start noticing the effects of my grammatical decisions on my own quality of life. As my experiment continued, this often meant behaving like a patient in a medical study and taking my soul's vital signs. Respiratory rate? I learned that I don't breathe as freely when I avoid use of the first-person pronoun as when I use it. Pulse? A certain way of managing the future tense keeps the beat steady, regardless of setbacks and unpleasant surprises. Temperature? Some grammatical moves—the use of ellipses, for example—warm up my relations with the people around me by implying tacit, shared knowledge, and I *feel* warmer.

Like my student who wrote endless sentences, I could go on and on in this vein: *It makes a difference* to my self-esteem whether I put a phrase bearing bad news about myself before the coordinate conjunction "but" or after it. It *affects* my level of hopefulness when I rely exclusively on forms of the verb "to be," which reduce both things and people to static entities. I have now recorded scores of such connections between grammar and my own well-being, some pronounced, others subtle. Conceivably, at least, every attribute a person might desire to develop—from decisiveness in an emergency to trust and generosity and the ability to tolerate uncertainty—stands to benefit from changes in one's verbal conduct, as I hope to show.

I have come to view the realm of grammar as a kind of rarefied gymnasium, where—instead of weights, a treadmill, mats, and a balance beam—one finds active verbs, passive verbs, periods, apostrophes, dashes, and a thousand other pieces of linguistic equipment, each of which, properly deployed, can provide exercise for the spirit like that which gym apparatus provides the body. Grammar can become a place to get in spiritual shape.

Several years into my self-study, I began to write short essays on my findings. The result is the book in your hands, an amalgam of reflections and very specific tips to try.

For a while, I wrestled with embarrassment about publishing a book of practical suggestions for enhancing one's quality of life by such novel means. Even with the help of well-established practices like meditation, no significant personal change occurs easily or quickly, and I didn't wish to imply otherwise when it comes to grammar's help. I think often of the lines in Philip Larkin's poem "Aubade" about each person's having just one stretch of years in which to live. "An only life," he says,

> . . . can take so long to climb
> Clear of its wrong beginnings, and may never.

Still, I've told myself, many people clear that bar when they find the kinds of help that suit them personally; everyone deserves to know what has benefited others. For the right person, that mere featherweight, a comma, can alter the course of a day.

Bootstrap Grammar—Taking Life in Hand

*F*ree will may be hard to prove philosoph-
ically, but its psychological double, sometimes called "a sense of agency"— the
enlivening impression that we're free and capable of
taking action in this world—seems to be a hard-wired
need. Human beings languish without it. Their states
of mind deteriorate. At the near end of decline, they live
what Thoreau terms "lives of quiet desperation" or
indulge in indirect, passive-aggressive behavior to bring
others down with them. At the far end of decline, as
researchers like Martin Seligman and Ellen Langer
have shown, they fall into depression, paralyzed—
bedridden figuratively, if not literally— by feelings of
hopelessness.

I think of the grammar in this section as linguistic
means for getting out of bed and "taking charge" of
one's life. That bold shift requires several basic habits
of mind, each of which I address in a separate essay
focused on a piece of grammar that fosters it. For example, one thing needed for taking life in hand is to practice believing (and insisting) that one has rights in this
world— and that's where the colon comes in.

Getting Noticed

Colons

If I am not for myself,
who will be?
—RABBI HILLEL

Quite fittingly, in English the word a speaker uses to refer to himself is "I," a word indistinguishable in appearance from the Roman numeral for "one" or "first." My first step in meeting my needs in this world is to *say* "I"—that is, to announce my presence and get noticed. I can't usually afford to wait on the sidelines for unbidden champions to do my advocacy for me. No one has as much at stake in my well-being as I myself do. Nor is anyone better positioned than I to name my needs or to say whether a given response to my needs satisfies them. I am the person who will pay most dearly if I can't sleep because of an all-night party next door, and I'm the one best qualified to answer the considerate partygoer's question, "Have we turned the music down low enough yet?"

Unfortunately, though, simply speaking up doesn't always do the trick of winning others' ears. When it doesn't, my confidence plummets and I start to doubt I have the *right* to speak and to be heard—which brings me to the colon.

The essayist Lewis Thomas found colons—those vertically arranged dots that say "Listen up; here's what you should know"—"a lot less attractive" than semicolons. "Firstly," he writes, "they give you the feeling of . . . having your nose pointed in a direction you might not be inclined to take it if left to yourself." But Strunk and White, the renowned authors of *The Elements of Style*, don't seem to have shared Thomas's aversion. In their own book, sometimes they use the colon to compel us to observe what can happen when a writer disregards one of their famous rules, an example being

Sentences violating Rule 7 are often ludicrous:

Elsewhere they employ it to oblige us to commit a rule to memory, as in

Punctuate as follows:

Those two dots have much the same riveting effect as the two loud clinks on a piece of fine glassware that announce a wedding toast—or the two decisive taps of a baton that call an orchestra to order just before a symphony begins.

According to E. B. White (the White of "Strunk and White"), Strunk "felt it was worse to be irresolute than to be wrong." He had been White's teacher in college, and one day in class he had "leaned far forward, in

... the pose of a man about to impart a secret—and croaked, 'If you don't know how to pronounce a word, say it loud!'" Strunk's use of colons—like so much else in *The Elements of Style*—bares the unapologetic soul at the top of its form. It says, "I have standing in this place, so heed me."

Which way to punctuate—nay, which way to live: that of the quietly respectful Lewis Thomas or that of the assertive Strunk? Can we do without either of these modes as we address the sometimes thorny, sometimes delicate, now and then clearly urgent situations lying before us? The first two seem likely to benefit from Thomas's tact; the last, from Strunk's display of strength.

In the belief that to live fully requires a balance in capacities, I favor equal readiness both to use the colon of command and to avoid its use. The best way for a person to achieve such balance is, it seems to me, Aristotle's way—namely, calling into play the side which, until now, one has not sufficiently developed, even if it means erring on that side a bit.

There are, for example, people who would just as soon colonize a foreign nation as "colon-ize" a sentence. To them, that two-pointed mark is a double-barreled shotgun; they keep it locked away. They might stand across the counter from the most unhelpful member of the staff of a hotel, waiting to register and to receive a room key, and still not feel at liberty to capture the person's attention with the speech inflection that corresponds to a written colon, as in

Friend, here's where things stand: Every fifteen minutes for the past hour and a half, you have been telling us our rooms would be ready in fifteen minutes. As a result, we have less than half an hour left to clean up and drive to our niece's graduation.

It's the colon after "stand" that lays claim to the air time needed to say the rest.

My father used to say, "Don't let people step on you." In his business correspondence—with which, as a boy, I used to help him, since he was an immigrant who never fully mastered English usage—he would insert a colon frequently, each pair of dots a typographical fair warning to the reader (the customer who'd sent him three bouncing checks in a row, the boss who had spoiled some of his sales through ill-advised pricing decisions) that he'd better not ignore my father's forthcoming words. Though I'm a fairly gentle soul myself, I retain the colon in my repertoire, and I suggest that other meek or mild types do so, too. We must learn to insist that we have rights to attention. That assertive punctuation mark represents one safe way to begin.

Energy

Transitive Verbs in the Active Voice

Not long ago, I was sitting in our neighborhood café when a three-year-old boy at the next table—letting his legs swing happily under him—suddenly stopped blowing his food cool (which he did with unreal intensity) to declare, "I feel like eating out today. I could eat the whole w-o-o-o-r-l-d."

A deeply satisfying rush went through me at his eagerness; I must have smiled or blushed in appreciation of a kindred soul. If the truth be known, I myself periodically dip back into that birthright pool of restless energy. At such moments I, too, speak transitively; I feel like *doing* something to the unsuspecting world—rousing it, taking it by storm, or fixing it.

Can the world's necessary deeds be performed by people who've lost access to that well of voltage? I submit a pair of sentences:

Working conditions at the office got better when Ted's request for a transfer was granted.

versus

13

In a single stroke, Anne improved conditions at the office: she granted Ted's request for a transfer.

To my ear, it is the second of these sentences which celebrates human agency. It reminds me that the individual—whether "Anne" or myself—still *has* agency. It does so partly by naming the agent, Anne. Also, though, it does so by replacing the intransitive verb "got better" (which is incapable of having a direct object: I can't take aim at a condition and "get better" it) with a transitive one, "improved," and by replacing a roundabout passive verb phrase, "Ted's request was granted," with its active counterpart, "granted Ted's request." "Anne improved conditions" has impact. "She granted Ted's request" has impact. Just reading those short strings of words, I can feel my blood sugar rise a bit. In writing them, I was energized twice as much.

Intransitive verbs such as "got better" and passive constructions like "was granted" don't oblige a speaker to say what or who is *responsible* for the act or situation described. The intransitive "The milk went bad" qualifies as a full, presentable sentence without ever saying what soured the milk. The intransitive "Max died" leaves unanswered the question "What—or who—killed Max?" Intransitive verbs as a class tend to reinforce the misunderstanding that things "just happen."

Passive constructions such as "was granted" do much the same: they produce a kind of throwing up of hands. In passive voice, the doer of the deed either makes no appearance in the sentence—as in "Ted was transferred"—or appears at the sentence's far end as an afterthought—as in "Ted was transferred by Anne."

One can spot such concealment of agency—or, in the lesser case, downplaying of agency—in much of the language issued by government offices (bureaus often known, ironically enough, *as* "agencies"). It sounds like this:

> A secret shipment of arms to the insurgents was requested on March 19, approved on March 20, and carried out on March 21. [*That's at least three different people who owe their anonymity to the passive voice.*]

> Undeniably, mistakes were made. [*Yes, but who made them?*]

In the world of medicine, concealment of agency sounds like the following excerpts from a note that a surgeon composed in 1961 at the request of the drug-addicted, dark comedian Lenny Bruce. It's a note written to assure "any peace officer observing fresh needle marks on Mr. Bruce's arm" that said marks had resulted from injections for medicinal purposes only.

> Mr. Bruce suffers from episodes of severe depression and lethargy. . . . He has been instructed in the proper use of intravenous injections of Methedrine. [*Who instructed Bruce? No one in particular?*]

> Methedrine in ampules of 1 cc. (20 mg.) together with disposable syringes, has been prescribed for intravenous use as needed. [*Who wrote the prescription? The same person who wrote this note or someone else?*]

I leave to others the ethical analysis of our verbal shirking of responsibility. At the moment, I want to consider how passive prose, which represents events as rudderless, affects the individual's morale. When I read or write such text, I am liable to feel powerless in relation to the situation being discussed, since I get no mental picture of a person engaged in doing something about it one way or another.

Put the examples above alongside this excerpt from a report to shareholders by the manager of a mutual fund in 2002, when stock values were plunging and he might have sought cover behind "forces beyond his control."

> In hindsight, my biggest mistake was shifting from a conservative mentality to an aggressive mindset prematurely. Within finance, for example, I added to the fund's stakes in brokerage-type names such as Citicorp and Merrill Lynch, and I de-emphasized conservative areas such as regional banks.

How refreshing! Just in reading those words—"I added," "I de-emphasized"—I feel incrementally empowered. As a member of the same species to which their author belongs, I tell myself, "I must also be capable of taking action despite risks." If I had written those words, the writing act—as an *exercise* in agency—would have had an even more empowering effect. I'd have been affirming, "Right or wrong, win or lose, my destiny is in my hands." The shareholder report was imperfect, can-do

America at its grammatical best. I almost didn't mind that the value of my Roth IRA had fallen again.

Psychologists Albert Ellis and Robert A. Harper advocate a therapeutic use of transitive-active constructions. They counsel their readers away from intransitive sentences such as

> My parents were the source of all my troubles and still are.

That sort of sentence, they say,

> serves as a cop-out for your past and present behavior. If you acknowledge, instead, "My parents kept criticizing me severely during my childhood, and I kept taking them too seriously and thereby kept upsetting myself . . . ," you strongly imply what you can do to interrupt and change your own self-downing tendencies.

We are not mere victims. Within certain, quite important limits (which I address in later sections of this book), we remain the masters of our own fate. Some verbs lull us and lead us to forget that fact; others keep it live in consciousness.

Wherewithal

Prepositions

Vic quickly found the chickadee.

Ruthie got her way in the committee.

Lynn attracts friends of both sexes.

Though each of these sentences employs a transitive verb in the active voice—"found," "got," "attracts"—each one could still go further toward setting in full motion the writer's cerebral wheels of agency. They stop short of naming the *means* by which their respective actions are accomplished. It's as if each one started with that question-begging adverb "somehow." Somehow, Vic found the chickadee. Somehow, Ruthie got her way.

Sentences like these call to mind the drawings turned out by many four-year-olds in which people have no arms. The young artist may inform us that he's drawn a man flying a kite, but all we see is an armless figure and a shape in the sky above it—no string, and no body part that could be used for holding a string. In its blindness to how the deed is done, such a drawing suggests that the artist is simply in awe; the idea that he himself could achieve a result like the one he depicts—an airborne kite—is inconceivable to him.

Agency demands an eye for means. In the realm of art, it demands (eventually) visualizing upper limbs with hands. In writing, as in speaking, it demands adding the *language* of instrumentality. It demands adding either whole sentences devoted to the "how of it" or at least prepositional how-to phrases—adverbial strings of words beginning with "by" or "with" and naming the takeable steps or known, available devices that make the inconceivable feat quite conceivable, as in

> By steadily pointing a finger toward the branch where he had observed it alight, Vic quickly found the chickadee again in his binoculars.

or

> By patiently listening to each of her colleagues in turn—and by calmly then addressing their misgivings Ruthie got her way in the committee.

Don't such phrases, which begin to break a new operation down into its parts, move that operation into closer range?

We can empower ourselves by adding limbs to our speech and writing, supplementing them with phrases of instrumentality whenever we recount acts worthy to be imitated. Any sentence that does no more about an act than to name it is a mere torso, not a heartening reminder of our wherewithal to undertake such acts ourselves, in good time.

Doing What Works

Anomalous Commas and Beyond

At times, the barrier to needful action is one's rigidity about rules. All states prohibit driving through a red light, and, normally, observing that prohibition has the effect intended: it prevents accidents. Occasionally, though, it can have the opposite effect. If the driver first in line at a traffic light that is stuck on red stubbornly refuses to adapt by advancing, one or more motorists behind him are likely to lose patience and move into the opposing lane in order to pass him. An unsafe situation rapidly becomes even less safe.

Likewise, schools have sufficient cause for their policies inhibiting teachers from touching students: a desire to prevent abuse. But taking these policies to their extreme—for example, by withholding a hug from the child in tears who has just been traumatized by a schoolyard bully—can look to the child like abandonment or even like complicity with her tormentor.

And if circumstance sometimes justifies violating laws and official policies, it can certainly excuse the occasional disregard of rules in the informal realm. I think of the custom not to wear white in winter. I think of people's reluctance to take silverware from a nearby unoccupied table in a restaurant even when their food is getting cold because their own table is forkless and knifeless. Rules and informal rules don't exist for their own sake; they're not sacred. Every so often, we must be ready to abandon a rule in favor of an act that would serve both ourselves and the world better. Because grammar is itself made up of rules—rules we sometimes need to violate to produce the right effect—it holds training value for us on this front. Going out on a limb with a low-stakes punctuation mark calls into play much the same dynamic that any judicious risk taking involves. In writing, as in life generally, it behooves us to override the normal settings at times.

Let's get specific, then. Circumstance will sometimes call for the insertion of a comma that the comma rules do not envision. We were taught to use commas to separate items in a series only when that series has at least three items in it, but that rule serves poorly in some cases. The following sentence adheres to that rule:

> Wallace Stevens wrote memos on questions of the
> insurance business and poetry.

Since the series in the sentence consists of only two items, "memos on questions of the insurance business" and "poetry," no comma comes between them. But without a comma there, the sentence can be read to mean that Wallace Stevens' contribution to the world of poetry took the form of memos about it! (And reversing the order of the items hardly improves matters. Try it.

The result is a sentence that can be read to mean Stevens' poetry dealt with issues in the insurance industry.) For communication's sake, we need

> Wallace Stevens wrote memos on questions of the insurance business, and poetry.

In addition, such commas can be justified on stylistic grounds at times. In the next sentence, Alice Walker ingeniously employs an unmandated comma for special effect, carving out *two* end-positions for the statement (therefore, two points of emphasis) where otherwise there would be just one:

> White men and women continued to run things, badly.

I propose a medical-sounding adjective for those who punctuate strictly by the rules, with no apparent consciousness of real effect: commatose. But, in fact, the comma rules are not the only rules of English grammar that a soul endowed with agency will break now and then. Scholars Margaret M. Bryant and Janet Rankin Aiken, writing fifty years ago in their book *Psychology of English*, rushed to the defense of a writer who violated the rule that singular subjects go with singular verbs, plural subjects with plural verbs:

> In saying "The tumult and the shouting dies" [rather than "die"], Kipling was utilizing the same

instinct which would lead a college student to select a matching tie and handkerchief.

Their implication—I agree with it—is that the words "tumult" and "shouting" may be separate and distinct, but "tumult and shouting" is a single phenomenon. A bit later on they write

> Only the myopia of scholarship can lead the grammarian to attempt to put grammar into a pigeonhole separate from living.

We must be at liberty to do what works.

While I'm at it, let me put a word in for sentences that are not complete. Yes, fragments.

"Yes, fragments" is, of course, itself a fragment. Does it confuse anyone? Does it even *distract* a reader? No? (There's *another* fragment.) Writing situations differ as to how much use of fragments will unofficially be countenanced. Push the envelope.

Revisiting the case of my defective traffic light, I readily concede that the worst, most lethal driver is the one who has no basis for knowing that the light's not working but runs it without waiting to find out. He probably runs a good many *functioning* red lights, too, when he's in a hurry. He is the person who flouts grammatical conventions as well, caring more about "making good time" in life than about either safety or sparing others a mess to clean up. He leaves to his secretary the insertion of commas and the agreement of nouns and verbs.

At the other extreme, however, is the driver so cowed by authority that he sits frozen at his wheel for an eternity, crawling his way out into the intersection only after others have begun to pass him on the left and, at that, feeling deep resentment toward those other drivers for their licentiousness. If I am right about him, he has never set to paper a paragraph comprised of only one sentence, or started any sentence with conjunctions "and" or "but" or "or" (let alone coined a new word), and his sense of agency in life could benefit from practice with transgression of just that magnitude and kind.

Lack of Time

The Imperative

Among the grammatical rules we must learn to ignore occasionally is the polite, wise rule against issuing orders to other people. If an electrician is working on a light switch in our front hallway when the front doorbell rings, it is that rule that keeps us from saying, "Get the door, Mr. Shay." Either we ourselves go to see who has come calling or we resort to less direct syntactical forms, such as questions. We say, "Would you mind getting that for me?"

Sometimes we must cut to the chase. Even in relationships based on strong mutual respect, occasions arise that call for shutting down the respectful instincts and shifting gears grammatically. They require the imperative mode of speech, in which the main clause starts with a verb, and the unspoken subject of that verb (the person intended to perform the action named by the verb) is always assumed to be "you." In the imperative we say, "Give me a hand here," or "Do it ASAP!"

Take the example of an emergency. If a woman has collapsed on a busy downtown sidewalk, someone needs to cry out, "Stand back! Stand back! Call 9–1–1, somebody!"

However, that mode of grammar and that decibel level represent a temperamental stretch for many of us. How can a quiet soul, for whom the shouted order is anathema, *get in shape* for taking charge at those inevitable moments when someone, herself or another, has fallen into harm's way?

Maybe she can start with emergencies that take days, rather than mere seconds, to play themselves out. And, in those cases, maybe she can start by shouting on paper, rather than aloud, since writing affords the would-be exclaimer a chance to get used to the sight of an exclamation mark before committing to it — a chance, that is, to *lower by degrees* her too-high barrier to shouting. She can start with notes to a spouse that read, "Don't forget that our deposit on the cottage is due tomorrow!" or, "Tell the kids not to practice diving in the shallow end!" She can go from there to honking when a car coming toward her on a dark road at night has no lights on. All that's left to activate after the writing hand and the car horn is the voice box.

Also worth noting: the imperative doesn't always have to be imperious. The four-year-old who's never gone swimming before may have trouble believing that a substance with as much loose play in it as water can hold him up. (I still marvel at the fact myself.) At such times, only doing can settle the question. We don't explain to that child all the science involved; we say, in the imperative, "Give it a try, you'll see" . . . and, of course, "I'll be right here to catch you if anything goes wrong."

The other times that warrant using the quiet imperative are those when enough is enough. We can't afford to let every last thing drag on in the effort to get it just right. One must, for example, occasionally say, imperatively, "Friends, we've been arguing for ten minutes about how to split the dinner bill. I can't speak for you, but I have better things to do with my evening. Here's a ten-dollar bill to cover me. Joan, Freddy, you put in the same. Kathy, make yours eight and we'll be set." Unless (a) the amounts proposed stray grossly from the mark of equity or (b) someone at the table suffers from a personality disorder, the entire group is likely to be grateful, even to laugh as they pull their wallets out. People know that some allowance must be made for the shortness of life.

GRAMMAR
FOR CREATIVE
PASSIVITY

The right shot at the right moment does not come because you do not let go of yourself. . . . What stands in your way is that you have a much too willful will. You think that what you do not do for yourself does not happen.

—Zen Archery Master Kenzo Awa,
quoted by Eugen Herrigel

*H*aving devoted the preceding section of this book to the theme of agency, I need to issue an important caveat. *Agency, the felt capacity to make things happen, all too often comes with a strident song inside the head: "I'm autonomous. Resolve is all I need for doing what I aim to; I only have to set my mind to it." That goes too far. To be sure, we can get things done (not all things, but many), but only if we join agency with its apparent opposite, receptivity.*

In tennis, if you keep a tight grip on the racket for the game's duration, not only will your muscles that produce that grip get sore, you will also play poorly.

Take it from me, who brought an anxious rigor to the game for many years: if you don't relax your arm between strokes, you can't reposition it to deal optimally with the next lob or slam to come your way. In tennis and in all of our pursuits, we need to readjust to details of the unfolding scene, or we can't be effective. We need to stay aware of our intent but also to relax it, in order to absorb the salient facts before us and their implications for how best to proceed. The "unrelaxed" doctor may not cast a wide enough net for possible diagnoses of a patient's condition—or may even fail to notice early signs of a complication his patient is having. The too-willful, damn-the-torpedoes entrepreneur may not give the weight she should to changes in tax law, market conditions, interest rates, or the availability of qualified workers. Even billionaire Donald Trump, whom the media have used to personify getting one's way, reports that he likes to have several deals going at once, "because most deals fall out, no matter how promising they seem at first."

The essay that opens this section will, I hope, lead my reader to attach a practical and spiritual value to the passive voice in grammar. In the end, however, it is neither agency alone nor passivity alone we need, but the two interlaced, as the last essay in this section, "Hybrid," suggests.

Getting Out of
One's Own Way

Passive Voice

A relative of William James once tried to explain passive voice to a small girl: "Suppose that you kill me: you who do the killing are in the active voice, and I, who am killed, am in the passive voice." (Here the passive construction is "am killed.") That smart girl was not satisfied, however.

> "How can you speak if you're killed?" said the child. "Oh, well, [said the adult,] you may suppose that I am not yet quite dead!" The next day the child was asked in class to explain the passive voice, and said, "It's the kind of voice you speak with when you ain't quite dead."

The theme of most commentary on the passive voice in our times appears to be its sad unfitness for use by writers who are not on their deathbeds. Strunk and White lead the way. In *The Elements of Style* they proclaim as their rule no. 10, "Use the active voice," and they press the case for "direct," "vigorous," "forcible" language. They don't favor the elimination of all passives; they themselves use the construction "can be made lively" on the same page where their rule no. 10 appears. But their thrust is clear: it is to inspire more writing like their own, writing that *has* thrust. (My essay above, "Energy," on the active voice, follows in their footsteps, since it addresses the problem of *needing* agency.)

By contrast, the grammarian Otto Jespersen takes a downright expansive view of the matter and manages to come up with five situations that justify writing in the passive voice. Often, for example, the subject, the doer of the action, simply cannot be identified, and recourse to the passive is therefore unavoidable, as in "He was killed in the Boer War."

Even the broad-minded Jespersen, however, does not see—or perhaps sees but does not cite—the spiritual possibilities in using the passive. Please bear with me as I blaze a path into that terrain. Consider these two sentences:

active voice
I won the Oscar for Best Actress.

passive voice
I was awarded the Oscar for Best Actress.

Think of all the factors besides talent that influence the members of the Academy of Motion Picture Arts and Sciences when they cast ballots for the year's best actress. A partial list:

- the pool from which to select (Most films produced in a given year get little exposure, even to members of the Academy, and actors in those films are therefore effectively out of the running at Oscar time.)

- likeability or friendship

- envy

- sympathy (especially for older actors who've been bypassed for awards)

- box office receipts

Which of the two formulations, active or passive, reflects more understanding of the whole context in which awards are made? The phrase "I won" seems to reduce a vast, complicated array of factors to just one (albeit a big one): talent—or talent coupled with will and hard work. It seems to say, "This was essentially my doing." Does the woman who says "I won"—even if her success indeed rests largely on her own talent—stand as good a chance to perceive her true bearings in relation to the world as the woman who, consciously or unconsciously, allows for the support and interplay of all the other elements that contributed to her success and says, "I was awarded"?

But I would take the point further still by suggesting that even if the actress's award were "all about talent" and owed nothing to extraneous factors, she might be well advised to account for triumph in passive terms.

Not long ago at a post-performance Q and A session, I heard puppeteer Eric Bass compellingly describe how, when performing, he "took his lead" from his puppet. And, in fact, his consummate performance had left me wondering who was in charge onstage, Bass himself or his wooden handful. "Art well concealed," you may say, and I agree, but there was more—an attitude embedded in the phrase "took my lead from."

Several decades earlier, the great actress Helen Hayes described much the same phenomenon to a reporter, who set down Hayes' belief that "the moment . . . she became more aware of Helen Hayes playing the part of Mary Stuart than of Mary Stuart portrayed by Helen Hayes—fine as the distinction is—the audience would lose the sense that she was a real character."

Artists of all kinds are surprisingly reticent to say outright that they create. When they don't call on the passive voice to describe their work—as in "I was inspired to"—they often resort to other ways to minimize their part in the process: "took my lead from" and the like. (Michelangelo talked of his sculpting as *finding* forms within raw slabs of marble.)

They have, I think, discovered something of crucial importance in all our pursuits: It takes a somewhat passive state of mind to obtain access to one's own best gifts; too forcible a feeling of "being in charge" drives those gifts into hiding. If that's right, we should regard the passive voice more highly than our language pundits do. It's an instrument of creativity.

The Latent Repertoire

Triple-Spacing

All clearings promise
—PHILIP BOOTH

Deepen your faith in passivity by testing the effects of it.

The novice writer and the self-described "bad writer," who have not yet glimpsed the countless word and grammar options that exist in writing hyperspace, too rapidly conclude that their first drafts on a subject are the best of which they're capable. When those frequently banal or off-target formulations ring false to them, they regret their having produced them and wish only to be done with the writing task. By contrast, writers with experience labor under few illusions about first drafts: they calmly wait them out; they become receptive, and their receptivity is usually rewarded.

I can still recall my first taste of watchful passivity in the revision process. In eighth-grade journalism class at Woodrow Wilson Junior High School, I was instructed to submit all copy triple-spaced, since it would probably require editing. I found the airy look of my submissions positively bracing. It was the look that says, "This amounts to but a single way of putting something that is sayable a thousand other ways. Play with diligent abandon in the oversized, expansive area *between* lines; unexpected, better turns of phrase will appear to you." And that spacious look almost always makes good on its word, as if, interspersed between the horizontal lines of type, the horizontal bands of apparent nothing were a great parallel universe of words and word structures, and all it took to see them was refocusing; alternatives come out of the woodwork.

In journalism class, I repaid that spaciousness with changes like the following:

draft 1, as typed triple-spaced

Last Friday, the Woodrow Wilson Eagles ended this year's football season with a big win, even though it took them until the last five minutes of the game to pull it off. By then, Coach Bagovicz had nearly lost his voice from shouting reminders at them.

draft 2, as handwritten between the typed lines and in the margins

With a mere five minutes remaining in the game—and with Coach Bagovicz going hoarse from shouting his reminders from the sidelines—the Woodrow Wilson Eagles scored the points that gave the team a big, season-ending win last Friday.

Here, the difference has little to do with vocabulary and mostly to do with grammar. A temporal phrase, "last

Friday," is relocated from the opening of draft 1 to the far end of draft 2. More importantly, in draft 2 both a long clause of draft 1 ("even though it took . . .") and a whole sentence of draft 1 ("By then, Coach Bagovicz . . . ") become prepositional "with" phrases and get moved so they lead up to the main point suspensefully—rather than trail off behind it, where they have no power to increase suspense. The improvement in vitality is, I think, unmistakable.

Accordingly, my concrete suggestion is to leave seas of space on the paper used for writing. Try my journalism teacher's practice, triple-spacing. Or try producing a draft by hand on a 5-by-7-inch pad and photocopying all the pages onto 8½-by-11-inch sheets, leaving great margins. B. F. Skinner once told me that he had such need of free play with his writing that he used sheets of paper 22 inches by 34 inches, a surface area eight times that of a normal sheet of paper.

With enough (of what I call) spatial encouragement, a writer can make all sorts of improvements. He can see a way to merge three choppy sentences into a single, flowing one that shows the logic connecting his ideas. He can see in an opaque draft sentence the potential for a more straightforward, lucid line, as Franklin D. Roosevelt did when he transformed

> We are endeavoring to construct a more inclusive society.

into

> We're going to make a country in which no one is
> left out.

—a sentence whose ordinary diction ensured that no one who listened to it got "left out."

I feel that my role as a writer is to find the realm of verbal possibility and lay it bare, to see what comes. And what I say of writing might be said of anything from gardening to scientific inquiry: By leaving open spaces in the work we do—and returning to them passively— we ultimately get results far more satisfying than our first, willful efforts produce. We and our work are enriched.

Hybrid

Blessing

Where does the elusive balance between proactivity and reactivity lie? In his poem "Ash Wednesday," T. S. Eliot writes, "Teach us to care and not to care," and those words express our deep aspiration to reconcile somehow the responsible (caring, morally "in charge") life of agency with the responsive, creatively passive life. As I've tried to show in the preceding essays, a person who does not learn how to have it both ways will fall short of his human potential. It may be true that

David Ortiz hit the baseball.

It is equally true that

The ball, hurtling toward David Ortiz at 95 mph in a vector that would, he could tell, pass through his strike zone, triggered his response to swing.

Unfortunately, English is sorely lacking in grammatical constructions that do justice to the hybrid state of mind involved in pulling off most real deeds on earth. Sentence after sentence, our language *forces us to choose* between active voice and passive voice.

A curious—and beautiful—exception is the formula that always begins with the subjunctive verb "may":

May the two of you know many happy years together.

May the road rise up to meet you.

May Nelson Mandela's wise, unvengeful leadership serve as an example to contending groups in Africa, the Middle East, and throughout the world.

What is happening by way of this locution? In each case, the speaker expresses a wish. But in saying "May the two of you . . . ," rather than "I hope the two of you . . . ," he or she seems almost to be exercising jurisdiction in the matter. The phrase "I hope" does only what it says, it expresses hope, but "may" goes beyond mere desire; it lends the whole utterance a sense of fiat or bestowal.

The blessing formula using "May" does several things at once:

- it identifies the speaker with a certain aspiration or vision, which he names;

- it implicitly acknowledges that he by himself does not have the power to bring the wished-for outcome to pass; and

- it invites the forces, people, or divinities whose help is required for that outcome to come into play.

If this understanding is correct, then blessings operate like Sanskrit mantras: they invoke. For example, by intoning "Kreeeeeeeeeeeeeeemmmmmmm," which is the sound associated with the Hindu goddess Kali, one calls upon—welcomes—that fearsome deity to invade one's spirit or soul and destroy the negative forms of ego to be found there. The welcome itself is active; the openness to what that welcome brings is passive. Perhaps the reason David Ortiz is good at what he does is that he always waits internally in a place of "may" as the ball approaches him.

Are there formulas blending active and passive in English I'm not thinking of? Ones that a would-be David Ortiz could use to activate *his* whole, active/passive self at home plate? We stand in need of them in all of our difficult undertakings.

For now, perhaps we should settle for the sort of alternation of modes practiced by Alcoholics Anonymous, one of whose tenets (on the side of agency) is to "make direct amends," while another (on the generative, passive side) is to "turn our will and our lives over to the care of God as we understand him." Perhaps the best we can do is to keep our discourse well varied, frequently mixing active and passive constructions, so that we both (a) become more faithful to the complexity and causal uncertainty of the stories we tell and (b) get ourselves in better trim to go either way—passive or active—to address imbalance at a moment's notice.

GRAMMAR FOR
BELONGING

*I*f, on occasion, we feel at peace with the universe, that probably has less to do with our fitness for a strange, vast, and volatile cosmos than it does with the reception we happen to be getting at the time from beings of our own kind, at home and in town. As Freud pointed out, in one's infancy one's mother is the world. Then society takes over, playing mother to us after we've been weaned. What Mom provided us in her own person during infancy is, in our adulthood, proffered on all sides by specialized others: for protection, we now go to the police; for affection, to a mate; and for milk, to the dairy aisle. Except as a member of a family—and/or friendship group, office team, or civic or religious institution—the individual would be hard put indeed to meet his needs, both material and psychic.

As I quoted earlier, Hillel once rhetorically asked, "If I am not for myself, who will be?" He did not leave matters at that, however, but unblinkingly went straight on to ask, "If I'm for myself alone, what am I?" And, of course, Hillel's two injunctions hardly contradict each other. To be "for myself"—even just to know my name and have a first set of bearings in this world—I require others.

That is, we human beings have abundant good reason for use of the first-person plural. It transforms me and other lone characters into a group—or represents my application for membership in a preexisting one. It is the invaluable linguistic move being made when a five-year-old boy—having successfully offered himself as a replacement for an absent peer, the usual fourth player in a game of foursquare at recess—proves himself adequate, then says, "We can play this way tomorrow, too, right?" With his "we," the boy boldly puts his isolation behind him. The same move is underway when a woman who's upset about crop-duster planes spraying DDT in her town gets on her phone to neighbors whom she barely knows and says (by and by), "I feel just as you do on this issue. We should organize."

"We," then, reflects the need for belonging—not just in a group but in the cosmos through a group. And "we" reflects the need for effectiveness where the individual alone, even if imbued with agency, has little hope of making an impact on the scale required.

Touch

Many Elements

The word "grammar" has such a civilized, orderly sound to it. One might think it can only address needs that came into being after the invention of the alphabet. Not so.

Our need for company, for instance, goes back thousands of times farther than the first written language. It's a prehistoric, animal need that survives in us intact. If, as infants, we do not receive ample doses of what transactional psychologists call "stroking"—if, that is, we are deprived of nurturing contact with members of our own species (picture chimps diligently grooming each other)—we are subsequently hard put to thrive in life. That's how we've been wired.

As we leave infancy for toddling, and toddling for elementary school, we acquire means to satisfy the need for stroking besides literal, physical contact. *Words* stroke us—almost any words, even "Excuse me, is that seat taken?"—if they're addressed to us in person. Such words represent our human world attending to us; we feel vaguely caressed by them.

Amazingly—and here comes grammar's role—we sometimes also feel stroked by the words of people we have never encountered in the flesh, as well as by the words of people we know but haven't seen for months or years. More precisely, we feel stroked by the illusion of their physical presence, the effect of intimacy created on a page when its author works traces of her *voice* among the words—the dismissive finality of certain grammatical fragments like "No way" and "Over my dead body," or the confidential tone of a parenthesis like the one in "He's a Pisces (need I say more?)." John Trimble, author of *Writing with Style*, calls this voice effect "warm, imaginative touch."

Nor is such fictitious body heat felt only by readers. Having myself engaged in some ventriloquism on paper, I can attest to its salutary effect on the writer, too. By use of voice, I, in a sense, reenter the space that my readers and I have shared physically—or that I imagine we share—anticipating their stopped breath or nods or appreciative laughter. I feel that I am doing more than imparting my ideas: I'm paying an enjoyable visit. I am keeping the sociable side of myself in good working order.

It takes practice to vocalize on paper. As Walker Gibson, a professor of English who has written extensively about tone and persona, explains,

> Someone walks in the door and we throw a greeting at him—or her. We can say HELLo, meaning I'm a bored and irascible fellow, or I'm kiddingly pretending to be, and O golly, you again! We can say hello, cheerfully, meaning you and I are friendly enough but not really intimate. Or we can say hellooo,

which defines, of course, quite a different speaker and quite a different relation.

In speech, these "hello's" are made distinct from one another through specific uses of the voicebox and face, which linguists have dubbed "kinesics."* "The trouble with the written word," says Gibson, "is that it comes to us without kinesics — no voicebox, no eyebrows." According to him, "The writer's task is to so surround his words with other words on the page that his reader may infer the quality of the desired speaking voice."

Making up in writing for writing's inaudibility is largely a matter of word choice — replacing "of course" with "sure, anytime," or (moving in the opposite direction, toward more formality) replacing "party" with "upcoming social event." However, punctuation and syntax play their parts as well. In fact, the modern system of punctuation introduced by the Italian printer Aldus Manutius (1450–1515) was partly an attempt to invest writing with speech effects, like pauses and relative emphasis.

Without knowing it, an anonymous fan of the TV soap opera *The Guiding Light* proved herself a more-than-worthy heir of Manutius and his fellow printer/innovators when, in 1982, she wrote to the show's producers. She put quotation marks around a word to make herself

---

* The Russian linguist Lev Vygotsky made much the same point by citing a long passage in Dostoyevsky's *The Diary of a Writer*, in which six young workmen manage to conduct a whole conversation using only one potent swear word but imbuing it with new meaning on each utterance through vocal inflection and gesture.

sound bemused, employed an exclamation mark to make herself sound surprised, worked in a two-word interrupter set off by commas ("you know") for a scolding touch, and even willfully misspelled a word ("please") to ensure that it got heard as she would have said it.

> Gentlemen:
> Here I am actually "hooked" on a program, to the extent of not even accepting an invitation if it means not being able to see my program!...
> The little lady that plays Nola Reardon is a darling, beautiful child—and certainly should go places. While she plays a difficult part, she actually makes you live the story with her.
> Puhlease—don't let her do any more damage. Tell your writers to let her mend her ways.
> Bad girls do, you know, and find happy solutions in their lives....

I daresay that by the time the producers of *The Guiding Light* finished reading this anonymous fan's letter, she'd become as vivid to them as some members of their families; they had had the pleasure of her company.

Fittingly, we also hear a live voice—a tongue-in-cheek, importuning voice, in this case—in the sentence that opens an article by college instructor of English John Dawkins, whose very subject is the rhetoric of punctuation.

> Punctuation—just one of the "mechanics" of writing, after all—is perhaps not the first thing you turn

to after checking [a] table of contents, but you
are here now, so let me try to keep you here by
announcing, quickly, the not unimportant claims
to be made.

Strange as it may seem, Dawkins' article provided me
with something in addition to the information I was
seeking when I looked it up. It presented me with
Dawkins himself. It was addressing a need just as basic
to the rationale for communal life as the need for information: the need for companionship.

In order to surface my own voice, I try to imagine
I'm writing a *letter* to my reader, even when I'm really
writing a report or a book. Private letters occupy a curious niche on the continuum from casual speech to formal prose. Yes, they are produced through fingers rather
than through lips, but because they're meant for people
we know, they naturally call into play our habits of conversation. I sometimes actually begin a draft *as* a letter
to a friend. "Paul," I might begin, "you ask where all my
reading about violence on TV leads me. Well, . . ." I try
to "talk it to him" on the page. There will be time
enough later for lopping off my salutation and the other
telltale signs that the first draft had been a piece of
correspondence.

Is writing with voice always professionally wise? No.
For audiences that (sometimes with good reason, sometimes not) persist in seeking a cold objectivity free of
human bias, voice is suspect. Writers needing a fair
hearing from these audiences would be well advised to

strive for the dispassionate tone of machines. But relatively few such bands of readers exist in this world, so writers are safe to be themselves in most cases. I have the proof in my hands: I have the post-election letter of a candidate to his supporters, where his personal resolve takes the form of a brief, deliberate silence: "I didn't win . . . this time." Even in the next item in my stack, a physicist's paper titled "Radiative Corrections as the Origin of Spontaneous Symmetry Breaking," the author's unique voice gets play—for example, in his use of the quirky, highly unscientific adverb "hideously" in the phrase "hideously infrared divergent."

If you care about fostering a sense of community between us—a sense of shared presence—don't just *write* to me. In your writing, be audibly the person you are in the flesh. Keep in touch, as they say.

Communication

Commas, Quotation Marks, Modifiers, Pronouns

*One should not aim at being possible
to understand, but at being impossible
to misunderstand.*

—QUINTILIAN

I have to laugh at my perversity in managing to get so far into this book without dealing with grammar's most widely recognized function, clear communication. I certainly never intended to neglect it entirely, since that basic use of grammar has as much to do with personal well-being as any of the less familiar uses do. When we miscommunicate, we get lost on our way to an event, take delivery of goods we never ordered, or fight for no reason. With every such failure in transmission, society becomes a bit less useful to us and, as we perceive it, less caring also. We feel "unheard," as we say.

We need to take pains to avoid being misunderstood, and that, in part, means taking pains to avoid pitfalls in syntax and punctuation.

It is no exaggeration to say we trade in confusion much of the time. A typical "day in the grammatical life" might begin with a *misplaced modifier*. A man—I'll call him Bud—tries to decide on his attire for an unusually cold autumn day, but no sooner does he tentatively don an old jacket of his than his wife says, "Being in such poor shape, you really shouldn't wear that." She means the jacket is in poor shape, but her word order leaves Bud thinking that it's him—or his belly in particular—that she has in mind.

When he arrives at work, our linguistic everyman is treated to a sentence with a crucial *punctuation mark missing*. His boss has sent him an email reading,

> Bud, I ran into Sven at the game last night. He said, "Bud's project team is reaching all the wrong conclusions. I disagree.

Bud would pay good money to know exactly where in this message Sven's words end, but the boss has not inserted an end-quotation mark. If the sentence "I disagree" is Sven's, it is Sven's way of underscoring how wrong Bud's conclusions are, and the boss, in letting Sven's words speak for themselves, is probably expressing concern about Bud's work. If, on the other hand, the sentence "I disagree" is the boss's own, it's his means of parting company with Sven and giving Bud a vote of confidence!

Soon enough, however, Bud is making contributions of his own to the world's confusion. To his assistant he sends an email containing a *pronoun reference problem*:

When Jane Hinkle comes around with her guest, Mrs. Singh from India, please tell Jane that I would like to see her.

By "her," he means Jane, but his assistant takes "her" to be the Indian guest. The mistake will cost him twenty awkward minutes later in the day.*

Then, as soon as he has hit the send button, our good man is out the door, walking in the sharp, brisk air between buildings, where he sees a colleague to whom he has promised completion of a project in January, when he'll be less busy. As they pass, to show that he has not forgotten his promise, he addresses a *fragment out of context* to her. Bud (reassuringly, he thinks) points an index finger upward and says, "January!" She responds with, "Yes, terrible." Soon, but too late, he realizes she has taken his one-word sentence "January!" as a comment on the weather, which is too cold for October.

It's not yet 10:00 a.m., and the wheels of semantic havoc are at full spin. (As if to reassure him that he's not alone, our friend passes a radio and hears the

---

* In the language of the Algonquin Indians, this pitfall, so common in English, rarely occurs. If a speaker of Algonquian opined, "The music of Norah Jones can't be compared with that of Lena Horne; she is one of a kind," the pronoun "she" would be marked as belonging either to Norah Jones or to Lena Horne (much as a party to a contract is referred to as "party of the first part" or "party of the second part"), and we'd know which it was. In English, we can't tell. The problem might be solved by replacing "she" with the name (repeated, that is) of the singer whom the speaker has in mind, or it might be solved by refashioning the whole sentence.

White House press secretary telling reporters that the president did not mean what he may have seemed to say the day before.) By 5:00 p.m., a veritable fog of words and marks has descended on the land, and the four common errors cited above account for but a small fraction of it. Other grammatical mistakes range from double negatives and tense shifts to egregious run-on sentences. Nongrammatical mistakes range from typos to the use of words that simply do not mean what we intend them to. Is it any wonder that the words *message* and *mess* are related?*

Sometimes the effect of our grammatical mismanagement is humorous. The headline writer who entitled an obituary "Chester Morrill Was Fed Secretary" would have us believe that the late official of the Federal Reserve Bank will be remembered mainly for committing an unwitting act of cannibalism.

Other times, lack of care with grammar does real harm. Consider, for instance, the woman who, in writing her will, decides to split her modest estate between two of her three children, since the third doesn't need financial help. She wants to assure the third that her decision in no way reflects the degree of her love for him, but the text comes out

> I will not be leaving money to Carlos. I am not doing this, because I do not care for him, as I'm sure he knows.

* Both words go back to the Latin word *mittere*, "to send" or "to place."

Without the comma between "this" and "because," this well-intentioned mother would have successfully conveyed what she meant to: it is not for lack of love for Carlos that she has disinherited him. The presence of that comma stands her statement on its head, making it say that, like it or not, her reason for disinheriting Carlos is that she doesn't care for him.

In wills, in the operating instructions for new products, and in treaties between nations, the gratuitous comma has sometimes caused damage out of all proportion to its throw-weight in ink.

On that cautionary note, I bring to an end my appeal for care in avoiding grammar's traps and snares. There is no denying the importance of clear, unobstructed transmission of ideas, even from the standpoint of our mental health and thriving, but I hesitate to give the pitfalls more space here for two reasons: First, the interested reader can find many whole books devoted *just* to them.* Second, I would like to devote most of *this* book to things more surprising.

---

* The main point of Lynne Truss's popular *Eats, Shoots and Leaves* is very much in keeping with mine in this chapter. Her book's title is in fact an example—remove the comma after *Eats* and observe the semantic difference.

Bonding

Ellipses

I think of the late, sweet folk-blues singer Mississippi John Hurt as the man who made the dots of the ellipsis (. . .) into notes of music. The first and maybe second time he came to a song's refrain, he'd sing all the words. In later repetitions, though, it could be hard to predict which of those words would escape his lips and which would be left to the listener's short-term memory as Mississippi John fell silent, letting his guitar sing for him. Sometimes he'd leave out the first or the last words, and sometimes he'd leave out words in the middle.

It always seemed appropriate that his ellipses be rendered as pleasing instrumental sounds. At its best, the ellipsis — that essentially grammatical move in which a speaker lets part of his intended statement go unspoken (usually without troubling to use the three dots) — is, among other things, a form of celebration, effectively a way of deepening community by showing that, to some degree at least, communal bonds exist already; some things that pertain to speaker and/or listener already "go without saying" between them. In verbal terms, intimacy starts and grows there.

At the shallow end of the elliptical pool can be found certain pleasantries. The complete, therefore relatively formal, distant statement "I thank you," becomes "thank you"—and that, in its turn, becomes "thanks." "I'll see you at Joe's house" gets truncated at both ends (as the speaker and the listener and Joe grow better acquainted) into the fragment "See you at Joe's."

Having considerably more bonding power than these are the "pointers": words and phrases like "even," "of all things," and "ironically." If I say in an email message, "Even my sister wanted to sign the get-well card to Mrs. O'Hara," I am using "even" to let my correspondent know that . . . well, *I* know that *he* knows me and my family *sufficiently* to know what makes my sister's act surprising; I don't need to tell him. If I say "My sister, of all people, refused to have wine," I am doing much the same; I am practically declaring my friend to be a close extension of my kin.

It is, to a large extent, the ellipsis which accounts for the celebrative, bonding power inherent in the telling of a good joke.

In a magazine, I once saw an impressionistic painting of a port in France. I liked it so well that I tore it out and decided to frame it. Only, it was laid out horizontally, and for the wall I had in mind for it I needed something vertical, so I cropped it liberally at both side ends, never considering that certain artist types among our friends might notice. When they do, I now say (in a tone you might term "staccato defensive"), "Hey. Look. It's a Monet. I couldn't afford the whole thing, all right?"

If, as I hope, a person laughs at this (of course, a person's *not* laughing suggests he or she is still fathoming the gaucheness of my act), that laughter's source is subterranean. It's in what my listener understands without my having said it—about my financial means to buy even a square inch of a Monet, about the absurdity of cutting such a painting into pieces in the first place. It's also in her tacit knowledge that in fact I am play-acting: she knows both that I'm lying and that I know that she knows that I'm lying, too.

Ever since embarking on this book-length personal tour of the world of English grammar, I have wondered at what port, if any, *love* would come into view. Perhaps here is where we get our first glimpse of it. In the most intimate relationships, a great deal (and sometimes, of course, too much) goes without saying. Foreplay is not always the best setting for complete sentences. As e. e. cummings wrote,

> [The person] who pays any attention
> to the syntax of things
> will never wholly kiss you.

I am now convinced that one of the most elliptical poems in English is, aptly enough, a love poem. It's by William Carlos Williams:

This Is Just to Say

I have eaten
the plums
that were in
the icebox
and which
you were probably
saving
for breakfast
Forgive me
they were delicious
so sweet
and so cold

What do we have here? Incredibly, in the margin of the book where I first read the poem forty years ago, all I say about it is "plums"! Just as the couple in the poem must have needed time to feel they could take in-house liberties with each other—and could even safely broadcast those liberties in notes on the fridge, as tacit proof of their bond's durability—I needed years of marriage to recognize that in this poem deep, abiding affection is, in part, what the poet seeks to convey.

Let's take our cue from the loving likes of Mississippi John Hurt and William Carlos Williams. Let's make rhythmically calculated use of silence to mark, revel in, and enlarge upon the good things that have taken root among us. That way, more and more of the locations we spend life in will begin to feel like home.

Being Correct

Apostrophes

The apostrophe? I hope I can stay interested in it long enough to finish writing about it. Of all the needs I name in these essays, the one involving the apostrophe is probably the one that least pertains to me personally: the need to learn to dot one's i's and cross one's t's. I already give too much attention to minutiae, the formal, trifling rules whose function is open to question—the invariable placement of a fork to the left of a plate, for instance, despite the fact that, for the majority, forks are wielded by the right hand most of the time. If I see a fork that has strayed rightward on a table, I discreetly put it in its place again.

The possibility exists, however, that some readers of this book err not on the side of *excessive* attention to custom's superficialities but on the side of negligence. The forks and knives they provide for eating might be found anywhere within a guest's reach. I address my short defense of correctness for correctness' sake to them.

What's at stake here may need spelling out. Not all grammatical mistakes produce confusion. Even in writing—where tone of voice as an aid to communication is limited, and body language as an aid is absent altogether—context often makes immediately clear the writer's intent. I am thinking, at the moment, of most violations of the rules for use of apostrophes. If I write,

> Those early computer enthusiast's obsession was computer games.

I violate the rule to place an apostrophe *after* the "s" at the end of a plural possessive noun. If I write,

> Sallys obsession was games.

I leave a possessive entirely unmarked as one. If I write,

> Her's was games.

I make still a different misstep. Yet in all three mispunctuated sentences, my reader instantly gets what I mean.

It would be tempting not to bother with details where intended meaning is delivered as efficiently and clearly as it is in these cases. Why fret and fuss where language satisfies its basic, communicative function?

To judge from the high percentage of times "its" and "it's" are used incorrectly now—the possessive "its" being spelled with an apostrophe like the contraction "it's" (for "it is") and vice versa—many of my best contemporaries *don't* fuss. Nowadays, "Its Halloween today" and "My bank changed it's fees for checking accounts" both seem to pass muster with most people.

The problem is simply that readers like me, who know the rules, still occupy positions that entail grading others' writing, approving or rejecting others' applications and written proposals, and hiring and firing others. In dealing with us, a writer who errs grammatically, even when his meaning is plain, pays a high price: the loss of what Aristotle calls *ethos*, the reader's good regard for the writer. After noting two or three errors in an application letter, memo, sign, or political flyer, we commence to wonder how competent and credible the writer is generally. Despite ourselves, we reason, "If the writer can't tell where to put a mere apostrophe, how can we assume he has tracked the ins and outs of his subject matter?"

Grammatical correctness of the trivial sort—epitomized by correct use of apostrophes—enhances well-being in the same way that correct behavior does in most social settings: lines at the cashier, meetings of a project team, track meets, parties, and funerals. It helps us to obtain respect, a fair hearing in this world.

One caveat: A person typically belongs to more than one discourse community. If we care about being in dialogue with others, we should care somewhat about correctness appropriate to each of the groups to which we belong, not just correctness in the eyes of the currently dominant group. There is no basis for believing that dialects like Black English, Spanglish, and Cockney are, as languages, any less adequate than standard English. My favorite pronouncement on the subject is still Max Weinreich's "A language is a dialect with an army and a navy."

Compromise

"They"—Made Singular

I t turns out that correctness is a moving target.

Occasionally, one of the undergraduate writing tutors I supervise at Bentley College puts an arcane question of grammar to me and I (if I happen to be at the top of my form that day) answer him at length. He and his fellows then stare at me in that same state of awe reserved by deer for headlights. Once, terminating just such a pause, one of the tutors observed, "Larry, you are like a god."

In the flush of glory, I sometimes neglect to comment that the so-called "rules" are nothing but reports of verbal usage out on the street, not the dictates of scholars like me.

I have yet to encounter the student adversary immortalized in John Barth's novel *The End of the Road*, a book whose antihero is a professor of English. At the moment of *his* encounter, this formidable teacher was feeling "acute, tuned up, razor sharp." He had just managed to explain "the rules governing the case forms of English pronouns"—why, for example, one should say, "I was thought to be he," not "I was thought to be him." Then, from the back of his classroom, his nemesis piped up with, "Aw, look, which came first, the language or the grammar books?"

> "What's on your mind, Blakesley?" [the professor] demanded, refusing to play his game.
>
> "Well, it stands to reason people talked before they wrote grammar books, and all the books did was tell how people were talking. For instance, when my roommate makes a phone call I ask him, 'Who are you talking to?' Everybody in this class would say, 'Who are you talking to?' . . . Nobody's going to say, 'To whom were you just now talking?' I'll bet even you wouldn't say it. It sounds queer, don't it?" The class snickered. "Now this is supposed to be a democracy, so if nobody but a few profs would ever say, 'To whom were you just now speaking?', why go on pretending we're all out of step but you? Why not change the rules?"

I can only hope that when my turn comes to deal with that challenge to authority, I display more candor than Barth's imaginary teacher goes on to summon. What the student here contends is mostly true: usage leads the way; rules come along to validate and stabilize usage temporarily. In other words: people follow rules, but only for as long as they please to. Ultimately, rules follow people.

In recent times, the ban against contractions such as "can't" and "she'll" in formal writing has been lifted at many print venues. Also, just as Barth's fictional student claims, most educated writers have begun to speak of "someone who I know"—kissing "whom" good-bye. Will educated speakers one day say, "That decision isn't fair to Josh and I," or "She and him went to the movies"? Quite possibly.

That's an unsettling prospect. In terms of personal growth, however, there is an upside to the never-ending story of linguistic change: it can be an arena for learning how to deal with change of all kinds.

Of the changes working their way through English right now, none is spreading faster than the use of the plural third-person pronoun "they" to do the work that logically belongs to a singular pronoun. The sentence

> A person who has undergone EMT training at Michigan knows what they're doing.

is likely to annoy a great many people who value precision in expression. How did the lone "a person" morph into that multitude "they"?

Of course we know the reason for this change. In the singular, English is lacking for third-person pronouns covering both sexes. The traditional solution of defaulting to "he" when the gender is irrelevant or unknown—

> A person who has undergone EMT training at Michigan knows what he is doing.

—has become unacceptable as we've grown more aware that such practices attach more agency and competence to men than to women. The readiest-to-hand substitute for "he" (other than "she," which simply reverses the bias) is "they."

Still, I resist "they" mightily. I resort to all manner of clumsier locutions to avoid seeming to conflate the single human being and the many. Maxine Hairston, the late professor of English who lived much of her life on a ranch, identified six nonsexist alternatives to "he," and in these essays I have used all but one.

- When feasible, use plural nouns and [thereby] eliminate the need to choose a pronoun of specific gender; often this is the simplest remedy. For example: "Painters who want to exhibit their work," not "A painter who wants to exhibit his work."

- Reword the sentence to eliminate the gender pronoun. For example: "The average American drives a car three years," instead of "The average American drives his car three years."

- When feasible, substitute *one* for *he* or *she* or *man* or *woman*. For example: "If one plans ahead, one can retire at 60," instead of "If a man plans ahead, he can retire at 60."

- When it seems indicated, write *he or she* or *his or her*; as long as you do not use the phrases too often, they will not be conspicuous.

- If you wish, consistently write *he/she* and *him/her*.

- Sometimes use *she* and *her* instead of *he* and *him* as general pronouns. For example: "The driver who is renewing her license must now pass an eye test," and "An officer who makes an arrest should show her badge."

Oh, I confess that in conversing with friends who freely use "they" in the place of a singular pronoun, I occasionally use it myself. I might say

> The accountant who pretends not to see blatant fraud does so because they're afraid of losing a client.

When I do, though, I always feel, well, not as compromised as the accountant in my example, but a bit compromised. The accountant fears losing customers; I fear losing my interlocutors as friends. My morale would benefit if I could somehow stop *feeling* compromised at those moments and start seeing them as opportunities for *learning* to compromise, within limits. The need to compromise is as much a fact of verbal life as it is a fact of social life generally. Like those famous arbiters of English usage, the Fowlers, I "prefer geniality to grammar."

But I say "compromise, within limits" advisedly. What we want to learn is not mimicry, not the smooth appropriation of locutions we hear on others' lips. To me (please excuse the bit of moralizing that I feel coming on), thoughtless echoing is the verbal counterpart to—and a preparation for—complicity in crimes of all sorts, ranging from teenagers' ostracism of a peer they deem uncool to adults' signing off, under peer pressure, on a product of their company's known to be hazardous.

Where, then, to look for guidance?

Maybe by tweaking some words by Eric Partridge on grammar, we can derive a principle that's not confined to grammar only. Grammar, says Partridge,

> must modify itself if language changes, grammar being made for man, not man for grammar.
>
> Nevertheless, where grammatical rules make for a clarity that would disappear with the disappearance of the rules, it is better to preserve and maintain the rules—until, at least, a more satisfactory rule [evolves].

If "personal standards of conduct" is substituted for "grammatical rules" and "humane quality of life" is substituted for "clarity," we may have the beginnings of a policy on compromise in general: "Where personal standards of conduct make for a humane quality of life that would disappear if one replaced them with new, more popular standards, it is better to go on behaving in accustomed ways until more satisfactory standards evolve."

At least, that's a working draft.

Trust

Exclamation Marks, Italics, Intensifiers

Many writers and grammarians inveigh against what I might call "typographical overkill," meaning the extensive use of italics, intensifiers, and exclamation marks to emphasize one's point. They see such devices as insults to a reader's intelligence. Consider some alternative formulations of a famous sentiment attributed to Voltaire:

> I may disagree with what you say, but I shall defend to the death your right to say it! (exclamation mark)

> I may disagree with what you say, but I shall defend to the death *your right to say it.* (italics)

> I may disagree with what you say, but I shall certainly, without question, defend to the death your right to say it. (intensifiers)

Writers who too frequently try to redouble emphasis by these means may well be better-intentioned than the boy who cried wolf, but they share his fate: their audience soon learns to discount their words generally and even comes to resent them. Of exclamation marks, Lewis Thomas writes, "Look! they say, look at what I just said! How amazing is my thought!" When he is subjected to these strident marks, he feels as if he's "being forced to watch someone else's small child jumping up and down crazily in the center of the living room shouting to attract attention." (Thanks to Thomas, I am now seeing in the exclamation mark—in the mark itself, its very shape—an abnormally rigid six-year-old, arms pressed tight against her sides, standing on her head for all to marvel at.) "If," writes Thomas, "a sentence really has something of importance to say, something quite remarkable, it doesn't need a mark to point it out."

A look at the Voltaire text undoctored seems to confirm the wisdom of Lewis's comment.

> I may disagree with what you say, but I shall defend
> to the death your right to say it.

The claim being made is extreme, but I'm likelier to buy it if, in his mode of expression, the speaker does not shout or bully me. Sober and steady in his tone, letting his sentiment speak for itself, he inclines me to listen.

The issue involved here is a fundamental issue of community: trust. I have tried to cut down on red-lettering in my own writing, but that's hard for me to do for the same reason that it's hard for me to delegate responsibility: I lack trust in others to "get it right" without my supervision. Though I know quite well how badly I react to higher-ups and writers who boss *me* around, the task of building my faith in others—I include you, dear reader—remains a struggle for me, one that takes place largely on the page. (For my most recent setback in the struggle, you needn't look far; it was the decision to italicize the first "me" in the preceding sentence.)

I've made progress, though. A case in point: In the introduction to this book you may recall having read this sentence:

> I wish to suggest that our list of activities capable of hastening personal growth be expanded beyond yoga, meditation, and the martial arts to include a wise use of syntax and punctuation.

But in my rough draft those words bore the imprint of my unchecked heavy hand: every word was italicized. Likewise, near the beginning of the essay titled "Touch," I ultimately cut back somewhat, settling for one hit over the head (the word "amazingly") in

> Amazingly . . . we sometimes also feel stroked by the words of people we have never encountered in the flesh.

where, initially, I had administered two, the second in the form of italics:

> Amazingly . . . *we sometimes also feel stroked by the words of people we have never encountered in the flesh.*

If you see now that, for want of the italics I deleted, you had not given these sentences their due weight when you first encountered them, you should probably keep that revelation to yourself, for my sake. I am thinking that by this time next year I may be able to delegate responsibilities at work, and to stop sending multiple reminders of scheduled events, and to forgo writing my social security number across the top of the reverse sides of tax schedules on whose front sides I have written it already.

Generosity

Semicolons, Cumulative Sentences

Not all of us possess the big heart we would like to have—the expansive, giving disposition that, from time to time in life, a relative or friend or teacher has displayed toward us, infusing us with confidence, infecting us with love of a game, a holiday, a work of art, or a career. Whether on account of an inherited "shy gene" or traumatic times in childhood that taught us the dangers that come with exposing ourselves to others, we may lack hearts of the right size for full participation in communal life.

Grammar offers two ways to supplement a personal program of heart enlargement. One is that mark of punctuation so inscrutable to most people, the semicolon. The other is a sentence form too rarely employed in this age of sound bites, the cumulative sentence.

Though John Trimble sings the semicolon's praises in his *Writing with Style*, he worries out loud that the average first-year college student "isn't ready" for it. As an instructor of writing myself, I must agree that college students seem to misuse the mark more often than they use it correctly. They understand its function as super-divider in a series of items that also includes commas—

as in "Tucson, Arizona; Fort Collins, Colorado; and Richmond, Virginia"—but its other, discursive functions elude them.

The following excerpts of Samuel Butler and Annie Dillard contain semicolons. I enter them in the record as instances of what that odd, earring-shaped mark means—at least to Butler and to Dillard and to me, if not to everyone: it signifies that one's largesse is not yet spent. I present Butler's semicolon first.

> We try to do with [words] what comes to very much like trying to mend a watch with a pickaxe or to paint a miniature with a mop; we expect them to help us to grip and dissect that which in ultimate essence is as ungrippable as shadow.

I draw Dillard's three semicolons from her account of a flight she took with a stunt pilot.

> I could not imagine loving [this pilot] under any circumstances; he was alien to me, unfazed.

> I gave up on everything, the way you do in airplanes; it was out of my hands.

> We dove at the [mountainside] headlong like suicides; we jerked up, down, or away at the last second, so late we left our hearts, stomachs, and lungs behind.

In each of these sentences, I hear the semicolon saying "which is to say"—and the clause that follows it elaborating on the text that has preceded it. In each, that is, the semicolon represents an unrequired gesture of amplification. It's a sign of being forthcoming, of being ungrudging in providing for the needs of others. I like Lewis Thomas's take on the semicolon:

> It is almost always a greater pleasure to come across a semicolon than a period. The period tells you that that is that; if you didn't get all the meaning you wanted or expected, anyway you got all the writer intended to parcel out and now you have to move along. But with the semicolon there you get a pleasant little feeling of expectancy; there is more to come; read on; it will get clearer.

A grammatical device with even more expansive potential for the heart is the cumulative sentence. To grasp its power, it helps first to recall that every independent clause sets forth a main assertion. For instance:

> Martinez will deal with his opponents' scurrilous attacks on him.

Dependent clauses can be added to the left and/or right of the independent clause to modify its meaning. In

> If he ever runs again for office, Martinez will deal with his opponents' scurrilous attacks on him more forcefully.

the dependent "if" clause that appears in front of the main clause, and the adverbial phrase "more forcefully" that takes up the rear, both modify the main clause—in this case saying, respectively, under what conditions and in what fashion the central asserted event would take place. Almost any independent clause can be extended far leftward or rightward in this manner.

Front-loading—that is, adding lengthily only to the left—results in what is known as a periodic sentence. Loading rightward, on the other hand, yields the cumulative sentence, in which, according to its chief exponent, Francis Christensen, additions to the main clause "modify the statement of the main clause or more often . . . explicate or exemplify it, so that the sentence has a flowing and ebbing movement, advancing to a new position and then pausing to consolidate it, leaping and lingering."

Compare the terse, ungenerous, cut-and-run effect of most sentences to the effect of the following cumulative line:

> If he ever runs again for office, Martinez will deal with his opponents' scurrilous attacks on him more forcefully, standing squarely in the middle of the fray, not malicious but unapologetic, handlers at his side who are ever ready with fresh, unequivocal press releases that enlarge upon their man's refutation of the latest trumped-up charges, all his political engines firing twenty-four-seven.

Sentences like that are overflowing, open-ended systems.

Here's a better (and less nerve-wracking) specimen than mine, by an unnamed student of Francis Christensen:

> It was as though someone, somewhere, had touched a lever and shifted gears, and the hospital was set for night running, smooth and silent, its normal clatter and hum muffled, the only sounds heard in the whitewalled room distant and unreal: a low hum of voices from the nurses' desk, quickly stifled, the soft squish of rubber-soled shoes on the tiled corridor, starched white cloth rustling against itself, and, outside, the lonesome whine of wind in the country night and the Kansas dust beating against the windows.

By the time I finish writing such a sentence (when I manage to), I can feel my chest swelling—not so much with pride as with a new, giving disposition. "One day," I fancifully tell myself, "I'll be as big a soul as that great fount of words and semicolons, Walt Whitman, whose generosity expanded beyond the limits of words to take nonverbal form as well." And I think of Whitman's unstinting service to the suffering in Civil War infirmaries.

Friends in the Graveyard

Present Tense

The dead who think
And live in ink.
—from an unpublished poem
by WARREN WEINSTEIN

When, a few years ago, I had my first excruciating episode with a kidney stone, my brother Warren, a lover of books, told me to reread Montaigne's essay on kidney stones, which I did. The sympathy of family and friends, though conveyed in real time by moving lips, paled next to the consolation provided by the written words of the world's first essayist. Of all my comforters, only Montaigne, who lived more than four hundred years ago, had had stones himself. Only he, for example, knew of the unusual euphoria that promptly envelops the sufferer on passing a stone.

I used my ad hoc consultation with Montaigne about our mutual medical condition as an excuse to revisit other pieces of his thought, ranging from perhaps the first influential call for religious tolerance in Christian

Europe to his lawyerly defense of a man's "male member," which opens with the concession

> We are right in remarking the untamed liberty of this member. He puffs himself up most importunely when we do not need him, and swoons away when our need is greatest.

As a result, phenomenologically speaking, Montaigne once again became a closer, more audible presence in my personal community than most of my contemporaries. In the words Montaigne himself uses about Tacitus, the Roman historian whose pronouncements still applied in Montaigne's own time, "You might often think he was . . . pinching us."

Some writers have lodged not only their ideas but bits of their actual text in my head, so that on relevant occasions—occasions proving those texts' enduring applicability—they are practically the first things out of my mouth. When I enter a new, beautifully designed workplace, home, or church, I frequently find myself quoting Hannah Arendt's "No activity can become excellent if the world does not provide a proper space for its exercise." When, in autumn, I first notice dried leaves flying in confusion up the pavement in front of me, I invariably say—out loud or to myself—Shelley's phrase in "Ode to the West Wind": "like ghosts from an enchanter fleeing." If I had no recourse to Montaigne, Shelley, Arendt, or a thousand other legally deceased persons—for their rare insights, as well as for their very sharp sense perceptions—I would feel an even deeper isolation from my true condition than I do in this strange world.

Others appear to have used books as I do. I think of the Cuban workers who rolled cigars to the sound of a paid lector reading from great books—a practice of the late nineteenth and early twentieth centuries dramatized by Nilo Cruz in his play *Anna in the Tropics* (where the Anna mentioned is Anna Karenina, whose story is the story being read to the workers). I think of the subway commuter who shuts me and our fellow passengers from his consciousness in order to absorb ten pages of Camus. I think of Malcolm X's awakening to books at the Norfolk Prison Colony, of which experience he writes, "Up to then, I never had been so truly free in my life."

The emperor Marcus Aurelius is said to have attended gladiatorial combat, the brutality of which he abhorred, only out of duty, and to have brought books with him there to read in plain view of all. I, in my turn, now read Aurelius as the world goes on around me.

We need means to induce such spirits to stay with us, revivify us, buoy us up. Are there verbal means besides quotation for expanding one's community to include the past? Yes, although the means that English offers for the purpose look small next to those available in certain other languages. As you may recall from the introduction to this book, Benjamin Lee Whorf believed he had discovered in the Hopi language a thoroughgoing mode of keeping everything and everyone alive at once. And the Chinese—who, not coincidentally, venerate their ancestors and ancestral wisdom—also have a language that blends tense, obscuring the temporal line that separates the dead from the living.

In English, we accommodate this need only to the extent that we permit use of present-tense verbs in reporting words or thoughts found in writerly texts—novels, poems, plays, exposés, treatises, and so on—even if their authors have returned to dust. Thus, we say,

> In *Rape of the Lock*, Pope skewers. . . .

or

> Melville's Captain Ahab is obsessed with. . . .

On the other hand, English stingily withholds a present-tense life in perpetuity from spoken words, even if they have great significance. We don't say,

> Neil Armstrong proclaims, "That's one small step for a man, one giant leap for mankind."

We say,

> Armstrong proclaimed. . . .

And we don't say,

> At about the time of my ninth birthday, Grandma Hlady tells me to think about the people who don't grow up with advantages like I have.

We say,

Grandma Hlady told me. . . .

Why not do what we can, however, to clear channels between us and the voices that are not immediate to us any longer, but to which we'd like to give the force of immediacy in our lives? Let's put Grandma's words between two life-restoring quotation marks and keep them somewhere near enough to hear them. To ourselves at least, let's say unabashedly, in present tense, "Grandma 'tells' me."

We attach too great a boundary-making power to the period of darkness called night, letting it define one small stretch of time, twenty-four hours, as separate from the next, as "yesterday," passé, discardable. In a real sense, it is still the same long day it always was, only later.

GRAMMAR FOR FREEDOM

I have known the eyes already,
   known them all—
The eyes that fix you in a formulated phrase,
And when I am formulated,
   sprawling on a pin,
When I am pinned and wriggling
   on the wall,
Then how should I begin
To spit out all the butt-ends of my days
   and ways?

                              —T. S. ELIOT

*T*he downside to being known by others is the likelihood of soon becoming a known quantity. T. S. Eliot's stanza on the spiritual cost of life in a community was the first snatch of modern poetry to surprise me with its resonance. At the time, I was chafing at the ways I was being labeled by high school peers. As I grew older, those classmates were replaced by coworkers, bosses, students of my own, constituents, and countless other specialists in sizing one up. To people who knew of my involvement in creating *a school desegregation plan, I was a champion of racial harmony. To hundreds who attended a meeting at which I opposed the appointment of a certain person of color to be the next principal of one of our city's schools, I was a racist.*

All too often, we take others' portrayals of us—even others' gross distortions of us—and internalize them, add them to the stock of lines we use against ourselves within our soundproof minds, where, unheard, their effects cannot be checked by true friends. In so doing, we become, to an extent, walking caricatures: the eternal Boy Scout, sycophant, martinet, housewife, whore. (What is the psychology of this acceptance of demeaning roles? Revenge? As R. D. Laing might say of schizophrenia— a way of giving one's disparagers yet more of what, apparently, they find so distasteful? Fear? As in, "This role, however ugly, I know I can play, having been seen playing it; other roles are probably beyond me"? Pure self-hatred? I am told that all of these factors are known to be involved.)

Because language plays a central part in the process of self-definition—and because grammar informs language—grammar has a role to play in avoiding and undoing the negative self-statements that are born communally, then brought inside ourselves, where they often do considerable damage.

Modeling
I-Statements

I n the heyday of encounter groups, psychologists devised what still seems to me a powerful linguistic means to keep people from confusing their reactions to each other with the truth about each other: I-statements. Rather than let one group participant say to a second one, "You're a threatening woman," they required all participants to refrain from definitional character assassination and to confine themselves, instead, to reports of their own feelings. "You're threatening" became "I feel threatened by you."

Generally speaking, we don't know enough about each other to sum each other up. In general, we do better saying how the other affects us. With I-statements,

You like to put people down, Bob.

gives way to

In that meeting we just had, I felt belittled by you, Bob.

Similarly, the you-statement

Sandra, you are one obsessive micromanager.

is supplanted by

> Sandra, I feel I need more discretion in this project
> than you've given me so far.

Books on raising children, such as Thomas Gordon's
P.E.T. [Parent Effectiveness Training] in Action, contain
many good examples. There, in the mouth of a man
whose four-year-old daughter doesn't understand how
their play together has exhausted him, the exasperated
you-line

> You stop pestering me now.

becomes the kinder I-line

> I'm too tired to play more with you now.*

Of course, the chief beneficiary of an I-statement is
the person to whom it is addressed, and those that ide-
ally would be addressed to us are not ours to make. We
want friends, coworkers, and acquaintances to know
better than to assault us in the second person. We want
spouses to know *not* to paint us into corners, telling

---

* A caveat is in order here, however. In the wrong tone of voice, I-
statements can prove fully as damning as accusatory you-statements.
One book on child-rearing surprisingly offers the following tirade as
a model I-statement: "When I see all of you rush away from dinner
to watch TV, and leave me with the dirty dishes and greasy pans, I
feel murderous! I get so mad I fume inside! I feel like taking every
dish and breaking it on the TV set!"

us, for instance, "You're no fun to take to parties any-
more," when, just as easily, they could use the first person to report their frustration that, at last night's party
when they'd felt like cutting loose, we held them back.
But we can't oblige others to know better, and some will
go on speaking as they have been doing, even after we
start talking differently to *them*. Still,

- we can model the alternative ourselves and
  hope for the best in return,

- we can soften (if not ever quite eliminate) the
  ill effects of others pigeonholing us just by
  noticing what they are doing,

- occasionally, we can take opportunities to
  call our accusers' attention to their definitional habits of speech, and let them know
  that we don't believe they do us justice.

Using E-Prime

The little word "is" has its tragedies:
it names and [equates] different things
with the greatest innocence; and yet
no two are ever identical.

—GEORGE SANTAYANA

The pronoun "you" turns out not to be the only questionable word in a definitional you-statement. It behooves us to take a second look at the verb that follows the pronoun as well.

Certain words and phrases correspond to signs in arithmetic. "And" is so close a match for "plus" that millions of people can be heard to say, "Two and three are five." "Without," "unless," and phrases like "except for" serve pretty much the role of the minus sign. All forms of the verb "to be"—*am, is, are, was, were, been, will be*—function as the equal sign functions in math. Perhaps this is why it took a would-be scientist, Count Alfred Korzybski, author of *Science and Sanity*, to lead an attack on our principal copulative verb. With a scientific zeal for precision, he pointed out that no phenomenon "equals" another. At least at the molecular level—and usually at the visible level, too—each contains pieces and aspects to be found nowhere else; each is complicated, each unique. Apple X cannot be equated with apple Y. It can't even be equated with itself (the same apple X) as it would exist a year later. (In Korzybski's words, a freshly picked apple "may be a very appetizing affair," and the same apple a year later may be "an unedible wet splash.")

If use of "to be" is problematic in relation to apples, how much more so when applied to us human beings, who somewhat exceed apples in complexity and unpredictability? Which is to say, the sentence "You are cowardly" is highly problematic. It is too simple, and it lacks respect for its subject's capacity for change over time; he's unlikely always to be cowardly, or to be a coward and nothing else. And yet the verb "are," a form of "to be," seems to sum that person up. I, in my time, have been told I was a disappointment, a hero, a lightweight, a genius, a progressive, a frightened middle-of-the-roader, and scores of other things. Every time a "to be" variant was wielded to define me, it gave me the distinct, paralyzing sense that my whole self had been encompassed. In each case, I needed to shake the new false identity off of me. Some came off cleanly; remnants of others unfortunately stuck, and I absorbed them into an enduring self-concept.

D. David Bourland, Jr., a disciple of Korzybski, became so convinced of the reductive potential in all forms of "to be" that in 1965 he began to promote what he called E-Prime, the English language stripped of *be*, *been*, *am*, *are*, *is*, *was*, and *were*. (The "E" in "E-Prime" stands for English. "Prime" indicates a variant.) He and associates like E. W. Kellogg III modeled it themselves, in speech as well as in writing. I invite my reader to gauge the difference that E-Prime can make. It is one thing to say to oneself,

I am a landlord now.

quite another to say,

I own a two-family house now and supplement my income with rent from it.

In E-Prime, the definitional

I'm such a jerk.

gets put aside in favor of facts, narrative that can be lived down, survived, and put behind:

I went and treated that girl rudely, I'm afraid.

In their *A New Guide to Rational Living*, a book deliberately written in E-Prime to model nondefinitional habits of thought, the well-known psychologist Albert Ellis and coauthor Robert A. Harper offer numerous similar examples, like

When [people] say, "I *am* no good at arithmetic," we get them to say, instead, "Up to the present time, I have done poorly at arithmetic."

A proper discussion of E-Prime would take more space than I have here. It has yet to be adopted by more than a handful of speakers and writers, and, to my mind, not all of its effects are as salutary as the one I've highlighted: undoing harmful self-equations. For example, it can make the use of passive constructions difficult, if not impossible. Still, its value can hardly be doubted. The college football player who, after a loss, is taunted by a gloating fan of the opposing team saying, "Hey there! Thomason! You're not much of an athlete, are you!" should reject definition and stick to the facts, especially in his own head, saying,

I had trouble completing my passes today.

or

For a third time this season, I fumbled the ball.

And that player should leave it at that. He should, so to speak, remain a free agent.

Shifting into Past Tense

Near the end of the preceding essay, the reader may have noticed that in offering alternatives to "to be" verbs (those verbs that, once internalized, take down and pin even the stoutest football player), I stick to the past tense: "had trouble," "fumbled the ball." My first discovery in experimenting with E-Prime was that, in itself, it did not eliminate the problem of verbal entrapment. We who care about our freedom from the definitional perceptions others have of us need to watch our tenses also.

Consider the difference between past tense ("fumbled the ball") and present tense ("fumble the ball"). For all the good E-Prime has done him, the resigned, perhaps depressed player who says "I fumble the ball" may as well drop E-Prime altogether and revert to the verb "to be," saying, "I am a fumbler." What we call the present tense in grammar should be dubbed the *present ongoing*. The actual present, that thin line dividing past and future, can't be rendered in words; any utterance attempting to describe it—even a play-by-play radio broadcast—is out of date by the time the first syllable hits page or air. (So much for living in the *true* present.)

In reality, outside of play-by-play or running coverage, present-tense verbs normally deal with actions and conditions that persist. Thus the football player who, using present tense, admits, "I have trouble with completing passes" veers too close to saying, "I am someone who, as a feature of my permanent identity, has trouble with. . . ."

To steer clear of such an effect requires the use of an available *past* tense—simple past tense, as in

> I *had* trouble completing my passes.

or past imperfect tense, as in

> I *was having* trouble completing my passes.

or past perfect tense, as in

> I *had had* trouble. . . .

Even the present imperfect tense conveys more potential for change than the present tense does:

> I *have been having* trouble. . . .

Compare for yourself:

> I smoke three packs a day.

> I have been smoking three packs a day since November, when my husband died.

I run on at the mouth.

At two or three events last week, I ran on at the mouth.

What's past is past.

Our Linguistic Limits

Her name was Magil
And she called herself Lil
But everyone knew her as Nancy.
—THE BEATLES

Good-by, Ruby Tuesday.
Who could hang a name on you?
—THE ROLLING STONES

When I began this book, I never imagined dwelling for so long on the topic of freedom. I had not yet looked about and noted all the features of language that effectively keep us in our places, unchanged.

Possibly the subtlest enforcer of the status quo is our use of proper nouns—that is, names. Because I have a name, I have a reputation that precedes me. On the campus where I've taught for decades, a veteran colleague of mine tells a new colleague, "You should see Larry Weinstein about your idea; that's *his* kind of thing" (or, in hushed tones, "Whatever you do, don't ever float that idea in Larry Weinstein's hearing"). My name functions in the way a brand name does: it assures the world at large of what to expect from the named product.

In ways imperceptible to us, we feel constrained by our names. One of the reasons we take vacations is to be among people who don't know us by name and won't be shocked if we suddenly act out of character.

What can be done about names, however? We need our names!*

When it comes to identity paralysis, I am hard put to formulate a good, comprehensive grammatical cure. All I can propose is those maneuvers discussed in the preceding three essays:

- I-statements (insofar as we can get others to frame their comments about us as I-statements)

- E-Prime

- past tense

They are enough, I hope, at least to keep the ground of

---

* In English, the only grammatical ploy that comes to mind for distancing one's current, whole self from past or partial selves is recourse to the third person. It's the path Shakespeare's Hamlet takes when he tells Laertes, whose father Hamlet has unintentionally killed and whose sister Hamlet's actions have driven to suicide: "Hamlet does it not, Hamlet denies it. Who does it, then? His madness." So, too, I can say of myself, "Politically, the post–9/11 Larry has some views that differ from those of the old Larry," or "I don't feel my normal, gloomy self today," or "You know only the wild Larry, not the sober, studious one. Tonight I want to stay home and read." Unfortunately, though, this third-person solution is hazardous. It corresponds roughly to what became known as "compartmentalization" during the 1990s. Taken too far, it can lead to wrong conduct with impunity, a life of aliases.

personality loose and arable, a soil still able on occasion to support new growth.

Near the end of a prayer known as the Amidah, Jews ask God to help them respond to their enemies—those who defame them, verbally reduce them—by letting their own souls "be as dust" toward their detractors. And the Hebrew word for "dust" (*ahfar*) is the same word used in Genesis: "Then the Lord God formed man of the dust of the ground." It's the vital stuff of which we're made. If all that the writers of the prayer had meant to convey was that one should remain silent in the face of demeaning misrepresentation, they might have used the simile of stone, a defensive hardening, but they did not. Wisely, I would say, they chose a simile not for ossified, inanimate silence but for life's silent source. The appropriate response of a person for whom others have invented names is not to stand stock still and thereby cooperate in her own diminution like a stone but to recall her ultimately true state, unnameability, and continue evolving.

GRAMMAR TO RESTORE THE EGO

*W*here the essays in the preceding section offer grammatical help for countering others' reductive distortions of oneself, the following two essays offer help from grammar for dealing with true personal failure. We need ways to maintain positive self-regard even as exhibits A, B, C, D, and E mount against us in the inner courtroom and we hear that more such proof of our incompetence is on its way.

Fulcrum

"But"

In the months following his graduation from Bentley College, a student of mine from China had several setbacks to his career. When I asked him how he was doing, he responded by telling me the story of General Zeng Guofan, who, in despair about the progress of a war, had drafted a report to the emperor reading,

> We fight, but the enemy defeats us.

When his protégé, General Zuo, read Zeng's draft, he proposed revising it to read,

> The enemy defeats us, but we fight on.

The revised text reassured Zeng's ruler and helped Zeng himself to remain in good spirits.

We are faced throughout our days with this grammatical decision: the choice of what to put *before* the conjunction "but" and what to put *after* it. Whatever goes last usually receives emphasis (grammarians call it *end-focus*), and the choice is ours to make; our language community demands only that both claims—the one that precedes "but" and the one that follows it—be true. By filling in the "but" clause, we exercise our right to declare which one is the more important, more salient or useful of the truths.

"But," then, is like a charmed fulcrum: put an army to its left, a feather to its right, and the feather falls as weightier. The power manifest in saying what goes left and right of "but" is, no doubt, part of what John Milton meant when he dubbed the mind "its own place," making "a Heav'n of Hell, a Hell of Heav'n."

Other grammatical means for assigning subjective weight exist as well. I think especially of subordinate clauses of concession — clauses and phrases that begin with words like "although" or "despite," like the "although" clause in

> Although, in the end, Cheryl wanted to stop seeing me, my time with her showed me I could get to be more intimate with someone than I'd ever thought I could.

As the terms "subordinate" and "main" suggest, the subordinate clause here houses the part of the story which the speaker wants to downplay; the main clause, that which he wants to feature and dwell upon.

If we're not to lose heart in the aftermath of setbacks or disasters, we must take care how we tell our stories. (At least one current tack among psychologists—narrative therapy—makes the revision of demoralizing autobiography its chief concern.) In her mind, the bankrupt entrepreneur can foreground either (a) the mistakes she made that led to bankruptcy or (b) the success she enjoyed for a while and the marketable skills she acquired as a result of it all. She needs to say, "In the end, I went belly up, yes, but. . . ."

Grammar,
Thing of Beauty

Sentence Length and
Repetition, among Other Things

*Grammar is a piano I play by ear, since I
seem to have been out of school the year the rules
were mentioned. All I know about grammar is its
infinite power. To shift the structure of a sentence
alters the meaning of that sentence, as definitely
and inflexibly as the position of a camera alters
the meaning of the object photographed.*

—JOAN DIDION

What can do more to enhance a person's
sense of self than having the ability to
bring into being beautiful things, such as
vibrant paintings or expressive melodies? As Joan Didion
suggests, grammar, too, lends itself to the creation of aesthetic pleasure. It should perhaps not surprise us, then,
that "grammar" is etymologically related to "glamour."*

---

* It was the association between grammar and magic (which seems
to have stood in people's minds for the connection between all high-
er learning and magic) that, through alterations in Scottish, led to
the word "glamour."

At its aesthetic best, grammar in some way mirrors the content of what is being said. For example, to evoke the suddenness of a realization, I might save naming the realization for the end of my sentence and spring it on my reader in a way that mimics how, in reality, it had hit me. I might write,

> There, out of airy nowhere, marching in disciplined silence past my feet, an interminable line of capable black ants was invading the house.

The possibilities for imitative beauty through grammar could fill multivolume tomes, as I hope the published specimens below will attest.

In the passage that opens Barbara Ehrenreich's essay "The Cult of Busyness," the news from a too-busy friend of hers is rendered as a rapid-fire series of unelaborated clauses, whereas the contrasting description of Ehrenreich's own laid-back "activity"—touching her toes—is fittingly presented in leisurely detail and capped by an idle, gratuitous appositive:

> Not too long ago a former friend and soon-to-be acquaintance called me up to tell me how busy she was. A major report, upon which her professional future depended, was due in three days; her secretary was on strike; her housekeeper had fallen into the hands of the Immigration Department; she had two hours to prepare a dinner party for eight; and she was late for her time-management class. Stress was taking its toll, she told me: her children resented the

fact that she sometimes got their names mixed up, and she had taken to abusing white wine.

All this put me at a distinct disadvantage, since the only thing I was doing at the time was holding the phone with one hand and attempting to touch the opposite toe with the other hand, a pastime that I had perfected during previous telephone monologues.

Of the Southdale Mall in Minnesota—the first indoor shopping mall, now more than fifty years old—Malcolm Gladwell writes, "It does not seem like a historic building, which is precisely why it is one." And to make his point that all other such malls, even the newest, are copies of that one, he goes on to use the bold grammatical device of simple repetition:

> Fifty years ago, Victor Gruen designed a fully enclosed, introverted, multitiered, double-anchor-tenant shopping complex with a garden court under a skylight—and today virtually every regional shopping center in America is a fully enclosed, introverted, multitiered, double-anchor-tenant complex with a garden court under a skylight.

To convey how rapidly a comrade in the Vietnam War went from being bright and strong to being dull and crippled, Richard Currey deploys at least three grammatical devices: He sticks mostly to relentless, relatively short, direct (subject/verb/object) sentences. He writes all but one of them in the present tense, even though the change being described took weeks or months to run its course. He disallows pausing by dispensing with paragraph breaks. By the end, we are made to feel, presumably as Currey himself feels, that his friend's awful transformation occurred in no time at all.

> Miguel Maldonado is nineteen years of age, a Lance Corporal in the United States Marine Corps, a first-generation Cuban-American from Miami, Florida. He is smart, funny, courageous. . . . He has, on more than one occasion, saved the lives of his fellow marines and platoon commander. He gets on with everybody in his unit, no matter their backgrounds, prejudices, religion, or politics. He has a natural inclination toward excellence: a soldier's soldier. He speaks of a career in the Marine Corps, telling everyone he has found a home at last. He is astonished to find himself successful and, despite the stress of combat, he is a happy man. It is in the last days of 1968 that Maldonado loses his right leg at mid-thigh and I use his belt as a crude tourniquet in the minutes before he is airlifted to the Naval Hospital at Cam Ranh Bay. When I see him next it is by chance, having escorted two wounded marines into the same hospital. There has been some trouble with the leg—a sloppy amputation, an infection— and Maldonado is medically addicted to opiates of one form or another. The bright energy and wide-eyed courage are gone. Maldonado knows he has entered the next stage of his life: a disabled Cuban high-school dropout drug addict, without prospects

or direction. I sit with him beside his bed. When I rise to go he grips my wrist. After a moment, however, he drops his hand. I say good-bye, wish him well, but he does not answer or look at me.

Does Currey's disheartening content disqualify his passage from consideration for beauty? Not in my view. Perhaps the most important aesthetic function is one Arthur Miller named: "to take [one's] agony home and teach it to sing." Rendering the awful beautifully implies that it can be dealt with.

The discredited but gifted author James Frey simulates how barriers came down between him and his parents (when they visited him at a drug rehab facility) partly by removing the normal barriers between sentences:

> We pull each of us pulls and we hug each other the three of us hug each other it is strong and easy and full of something maybe love.

By varying the length of whole sentences, Annie Dillard carries us aloft with a bird she spots imitating stunt pilots at an air show. She begins,

> The show was over. It was late.

That is, a sentence of four words is followed by a sentence of three words, as much to say, "Closing time. Everybody out." But then, in keeping with her subject, the number of words per sentence soars again:

Just as I turned from the runway, something caught my eye and made me laugh. It was a swallow, having its own air show, apparently inspired by [stunt pilot] Rahm. The swallow climbed high over the runway, held its wings oddly, tipped them, and rolled down the air in loops.

Jimi Hendrix found potential for expressive beauty in feedback from his amp. (I think in particular of his "Star Spangled Banner," with its eerily whistling "bombs bursting in air.") Hip-hop artists found the same in the sound of a needle scratching vinyl. Should we expect less from a storehouse of effects as vast as grammar?

Much as loop-de-loops and nosedives lit a fire under Annie Dillard's swallow, the maneuvers of writers like Dillard can inspire *us* to feats that enlarge our estimation of ourselves.

GRAMMAR FOR MINDFULNESS

You shall no longer take
things at second or third hand,
nor look through the eyes of the dead.
—WALT WHITMAN

Existentialism means no one
else can take a bath for you.
—DELMORE SCHWARTZ

*T*he most sacred utterance of the Jewish lit-
urgy is the Shema:

Hear, O Israel:
the Lord our God, the Lord is One.

In keeping with published translations of the Bible, I
insert a colon, as you can see, after the noun of address
"Israel," since what follows is a declaration. Even so, for
more than thirty years, I have wondered which way the
colon points us—back to the speaker or outward to the
world the speaker beholds. Is he enjoining the people to
heed what he himself is about to say, or is he implor-
ing them to open their ears to all that surrounds
them? Are the words "the Lord is One" an article of
faith he wants them to take from his own lips? Or,
much differently, are they his report of what they'll hear
for themselves if they but attend to the creation?

I prefer to think the latter, to believe my tradition values a direct, fresh response to the world here and now—that is, mindfulness. After all, one thing required for a full life is to be alive in the first place—to be open to the universe in detail, to notice it. I want to notice that the flooding a spring rain produced has turned an unremarkable low hill on campus into a genuine island for a day. I want to notice how a dozen fresh-cut tulips on the kitchen table open, close, and move from side to side in response to the sunlight.

We need our five good senses for the purpose. If, on a hurried walk to do an errand, I am suddenly confronted by a long, stopped freight train blocking my way at a crossing, I don't want to think only of how late I'll be: that would close my nose, eyes, and ears to the huge, unexpected marvel before me, a train. I would not, for example, hear (possibly for my first time) noises that a stopped train makes announcing that the behemoth's resumption of movement is imminent: the hiss of a brake under each car and, more dramatically, a distant, metal-on-metal clanking that rapidly gets louder as the couplings between cars (which went slack when the train first stopped) come taut again, one after another in strict order from the front, as the engine once again pulls forward. If I were to give my lateness too much of my finite attention, I would miss the thrill of seeing that the loudest clank of all coincides with the instant when the freight car closest to me stops being sedentary.

I feel much the same about ideas. With our minds too committed to one "take" on a question—for example, how best to perform a routine function at work—we make poor listeners at the times when others try to introduce us to new, divergent thoughts on the subject. In the inattentive frame of mind, we see both the unanticipated freight train and the unanticipated train of thought merely as nuisances.

What has grammar got to do with mindfulness? Quite a lot. I count at least two tenacious mental habits that obstruct mindfulness:

- *We forget how ignorant we are. (Why bother taking things in if we already have the world down pat?)*
- *We commit ourselves to plans (like the plan to do an errand quickly, in the freight train case) and become preoccupied with seeing them through to the end, regardless of what unfolds around us in the meantime.*

If I'm right, our use of grammar has helped get us into these confining mindsets, and it can help extricate us from them. The first two essays in this section provide grammatical antidotes to false certainty; the third, an antidote to preoccupation.

Speaking Without Feigning Certainty: Part I

Avoiding the Third-Person Omniscient

We commonly do not remember that it is, after all, always the first person that is speaking.

—HENRY DAVID THOREAU

By the time I meet students at the college level, many have taken to heart the rule never to say "I" in their papers. Their instructors have told them, "It's your writing. Your reader assumes the ideas in it are yours." One wonders if those instructors are aware that no less revered a writer than Thoreau used "I" in *Walden* 1,811 times, according to someone who has taken the time to count.

I can sympathize with the impulse to correct prose top-heavy with first-person pronouns, which suggests that all the young writer requires for support of an idea is her belief in it. Here is what that sounds like:

> I don't feel this school needs an honor code. I believe
> most students want to do the right thing already. To
> me, we should be left to our own instincts for mon-
> itoring cheating on campus. This is my position on
> the issue.

On the other hand, the policy of *never* saying "I"
(or "me" or "my") also produces troubling results—
including the adoption of an unreal voice, third-person
omniscient, which omits the signs of human fallibility.
"I believe most students want to do the right thing
already" turns into the conclusive "Most students want
to do the right thing already." In grammatically erasing
ourselves from what we say, we encourage others to
regard us as spokespersons for established truth. If
we get too good at it, we eventually *become* the cock-
sure spirits we impersonate, and mindfulness plummets. We see the tangible "facts on the ground" dimly,
if at all.

During the years when my brother and I were
teenagers, my mother found herself surrounded by my
father and my brother and me, three know-it-all males.
Her way to discount our pronouncements on the issues
of the day (for example, whether either of the two
superpowers of that time would ever launch a nuclear
attack on the other) was to hear us out, nodding all the
while even if she wasn't listening, and to add "In. Your.
Opinion." This invariable tagline of hers always tended
(after it was done provoking laughter from bystanders)
to put me back in touch with the impostor in me and

to incline me to give opposing points of view a better hearing.

The enemy of knowledge is certainty.

Speaking Without Feigning Certainty: Part II

Emily Dickinson's Dashes

Emily Dickinson unsettles her readers with her punctuation. At hundreds of points that you and I would have thought called for commas or periods or nothing at all, Dickinson puts dashes.

> Pain—has an Element of Blank—
> It cannot recollect
> When it begun—or if there were
> A time when it was not—

Of Dickinson's mechanics, her first editor, Thomas Wentworth Higginson, wrote, "When a thought takes one's breath away, a lesson on grammar seems an impertinence." But her dashes, those intrusive horizontal lines of ink, so annoyed Higginson and other early editors of the poems that they took it upon themselves to delete and replace many of them at the same time they were making other changes. The original printing of the above stanza, edited by Higginson and Mabel Loomis Todd, reads (I might say sedately reads)

Pain has an element of blank;
It cannot recollect
When it began, or if there were
A day when it was not.

Scholars have propounded several theories to explain—or explain away—Dickinson's dashes. One features their rhythmic value, another their ability to bring ostensibly unrelated words into relation with each other. R. W. Franklin dismisses the poet's use of them as a mere "habit of handwriting," pointing out the many that appear in a recipe of hers that has come down to us.

Myself, I prefer to believe that Dickinson's reasons have something to do with lack of sure knowledge. "Don't dwell too long on my words," she seems to be saying, "I have achieved no closure through them, only fleeting respite.* They are just the latest words to come to me; I literally dashed them off." (I conceive her writing the stanza on pain in the midst of an excruciating toothache or migraine, each dash representing her attempt to wrest a bit of meaning from the throbbing that assailed her.) Such a subtext, which disclaims all rights to immortality, would fit with facts we know about Dickinson the writer: her not troubling to title her poems, her putting only minimal effort into publishing them.

---

* What her fellow New England poet Robert Frost called "a momentary stay against confusion."

It's as if the same poet who strove to "Tell . . . the truth, but tell it slant"—so as not to blind herself or others in the process—had, for much the same reason, taken the additional motto, "Tell the truth, but tell it on the run." Dickinson effectively *streaks* by on the page. Only King Lear in his madness on the heath, and this poet secluded in her room, seem always to have biting cold winds in their hair.

Too extreme a use of punctuation in the cause of signaling alertness to the real, passing moment? Possibly. But she was a very alert, alive human being. One enlivening practice available to us is Dickinson's custom of imprinting on a text its nature as a work in progress. It doesn't matter if we do that with dashes or by more respectable means—such as question marks and speculative language ("maybe," "it would seem to me right now," etc.): In speaking less assuredly, we become more wide-awake.

Every one of Dickinson's quarter-inch-long horizontal marks is, if I am right, a disclaimer in the service of mindfulness. As Leonard Cohen tells us in one of his songs, "There is a hole in everything. That's how the light gets in."

Checking Preoccupation

Future Tense and Adverbial Provisos

That auxiliary verb "will," the signature of most plans, launches us into a new time zone. In so doing, it's both salvation and curse.

I readily concede that "will" is our principal supplier of hope, and that life depends on it. I think of the many times when private individuals like you and me employ "will" to rally in the face of private troubles. "We'll pull through," we say, "We will." I think also of Winston Churchill's use of "will" in the dark early days of World War II, and of Rudy Giuliani's use of "will" amid the ominous debris—still smoking—that was all that remained of the World Trade Center on September 11, 2001. By projecting mental pictures of ourselves forward in time, we keep *moving* forward; it's those images that give us the animating confidence we need to fight back or rebuild.

"Will" is justified at countless other, less dire moments, too. We call upon it with good reason for thousands of purposes that can't be achieved *except* through commitment over time: learning Spanish, saving enough money to buy a first home, writing a book like this one.

The problem with "I will" is that, in saying it (or its contracted form, "I'll"), we stake ourselves; we drive a promise into the ground, like a flagpole, and invite the world to hold us to account for the result.

> I'll repaint my room today.

> Stop worrying about the wedding; I will see to everything.

The burden, even in these un-Churchillian scenarios, is actually enormous, if we believe we're saying "It's as good as done." In order not to fail at the work "will" commits us to, we minimize awareness of anything in the environment that might distract us until it's finished. We put blinders on. We immerse ourselves in seeing our plans through, even though, to do so, we miss sights and sounds, opportunities, and sometimes even crises that occur nearby. We have no mental space for them; we're preoccupied.

In this way, plan-making is as big an obstacle to mindfulness as feigned certainty.

The question is one of degree. If we are to keep commitments, we must, to some extent, narrow our sights. But must our necessary blinders be perfectly opaque, letting in no light or image whatsoever, except for the path we're embarked on? It may be true that few of us are as unmindful as the inmate on Death

Row, depicted in a cartoon, who declines the offer of a sweet dessert for his last meal because, he says, he is on a low-carb diet. Yet many of the rest of us become so thoroughly seduced and enveloped by the future we have promised ourselves—a trimmer physique, as in the inmate's case, or a newly painted room, or a lovely wedding—that we lose touch with what lies palpably at hand.

One small grammatical adjustment has lessened my own tendency to let plans monopolize my consciousness. It is to work into my speech and writing adverbial qualifiers like:

> if things go on schedule,
> barring unforeseen developments,
> [or, for the religious] God willing.

I say, "Unless other, more important things come up, I'll repaint my room today."

A modest grammatical step, I grant. But I credit it, in part, with the fact that over time my peripheral vision has improved. I see more at the margins of my planned life.

I am especially pleased with my progress at the moment. I just got back from a hike that was part of a plan—a plan to solve a problem by thinking it out today. But I had told myself, as I laced my hiking boots, "I'll devote my attention during the entire hike to this plan . . . unless something new or anomalous catches my eye along the trail, and it seems worth a brief intermission." That qualifier was enough. As I passed a tree that had been stripped—stripped overnight, I would have said—of half its leaves, I observed a kind of frenzied pile-up of moth caterpillars on a branch near me. I took note of one that scrambled over one of its stalled siblings to find a less congested, faster route to the disappearing foliage that still remained. I took note, as well, of that tree's immobility, which rendered it defenseless in the onslaught. Then, but only then—after absorbing an all-too-vivid proof of Nature's amorality— did I continue on my way, letting the day's work resume its claim on my consciousness.

A Digression on the Spiritual Value of Dictionaries

All that you need to recall in order to follow my story is this: At the upper two corners of each page of a dictionary, one finds two words. By convention, typesetters give top left-hand billing to the entry that happens to appear first on the page, top right-hand billing to the entry that happens to appear last on it.

I can't remember what word I was looking for one day, but in the process I stumbled on the right-hand guideword of page 510 of *Webster's Seventh New Collegiate Dictionary*. It was "make love." Since few signposts ring so much of exhortation, I was briefly amused. Also, I was mildly surprised to find "make love" in the dictionary at all and therefore took an extra moment to locate and read the entry for it. The entry existed all right—only not where it should have, last on the page. For this once, despite the dictionary editors' guiding principle of impartiality, a typesetter had managed to promote his own view of life at the dictionary's expense, willfully lifting into prominence not the last word on a page but a phrase drawn from the page's middle that had special meaning to him.

How did I respond to the typesetter's prank? I proved myself as capable of preoccupation as the typesetter was. I took my juicy bit of lexical gossip and obsessed myself with it, played it—in my head at first, and then before the world—for all it might be worth, to the full exclusion of a lot else. The country might have gone to war without my noticing it.

I mostly set my piqued imagination loose on the typesetter culprit. Who, exactly, *was* this person giving me unsolicited advice—telling me behind his superiors' backs to go and "make love"? No doubt, I thought, he was a young man. He had tried college briefly, dropped out, was currently sharing his apartment with a girl who had never been so brainwashed as to enroll at college in the first place. He and she did little talking, were of the same one inclination: to indulge sensually. He raised his half of the rent by typesetting, that being the first opportunity to come his way; she, hers, by waitressing or temping. In the moment inspiration struck him, he had laughed out loud, though in the presence of other typesetters. When one of them had eyed him and asked, "Hey, so what's the big joke?" he had exulted, "Nothing! Absolutely nothing!" He cared little for holding down a particular job, even less for the business of listing words. Should he have been fired for his mischief, he would have counted it no great loss. And if all went unnoticed through to publication, he would have been able to claim a covert early victory in the society-wide conflict of lifestyles that he saw looming.

Soon my wife, my colleagues, and my neighbors knew of what I had unearthed. I was playing archaeologist to the hilt. "What intrigues me," I would say, "is the question of human types: To which human type does our perpetrator belong? As I have come to view him, . . ."

There was a plot twist, though. I didn't see it coming. Webster's compilation was about to introduce me to a way that any dictionary benefits well-being, if used properly.

When I'd gotten all the mileage I could out of "make love," I went back to look for other such breaches of lexical conduct. Certainly many more than one typesetter work on a project the size of a dictionary, and they all have private causes—free love, cheese, stocks and bonds, the tango, Ayn Rand. . . . Human nature being what it is, there had to have been more than one instance of mischief in the print shop.

But no, insofar as I could tell, there had only been that one. Otherwise, the English-speaking world's authoritative catalogue of words remained the same well-ventilated bulwark against undue fixation it had always been, from "aardvark" through the far-off, sparsely populated z's, a sublimely nonjudgmental repository of all life's possibilities, no more committed to "sex" or to "scholarship" than to the "saxophone." I could almost hear it whisper to me as I turned its pages: "Turn. Turn. Turn to next things. Keep turning." It all but quoted from Ecclesiastes, "There's a time to every purpose under heaven."

As I went on browsing, I could actually feel my preoccupation lifting. I heard birds and street sounds and took note of unopened mail. It occurred to me that a dictionary, by design, is intended not to capture our attention and draw it away from awareness of the moment; it is intended to preserve us from capture.

Now, periodically, I keep at hand a dictionary (one other than the tainted *Webster's Seventh New Collegiate*, which is out of print, in any case) — to counteract whatever my current obsession may be. If only for five minutes, I permit that thick, plotless book to quietly support a latent openness in me to new developments. After looking up a word, I let several unrelated entries catch my eye and I read them, to recall that there is still a "great big world out there." When I set the dictionary down again, I am, for a while at least, more alive to my surroundings.

Tolerating Ambiguity

"And"

I see now that by the time you reach this book's last page, dear reader, you will have been treated to several contradictory ideals. To achieve a form of agency infused with passivity . . . to join wholeheartedly in one's community without allowing it the power to define oneself . . . to be and not to be immersed in plans for the future. . . . Can I, can you, really hold in mind, let alone bring whole into our conduct, such paradoxical longings?

In my twenties, I read — rather, tried to read — William Empson's *Seven Types of Ambiguity*, in which Empson quotes numerous passages from English literature that can be construed in more than one way, classifying each. One, for example, is a case of "second-type ambiguity," where "two or more alternative meanings are fully resolved into one"; another is a case of "third-type ambiguity," where "two apparently *unconnected* meanings are given simultaneously" (italics mine). I found Empson's book intriguing but exasperating. Much of his prose was abstruse. I simply couldn't tell how certain of his categories differed in the least from certain other ones. And through it all, I wondered: Why bother? Even where, as in most of Empson's sampling, ambiguity reflects not sloppiness but authorial intention, what can be said of it beyond its being clever?

It was not until his last chapter that I heard Empson address that question, and he did so in such a fleeting, offhand manner that for thirty years afterward I imagined that his sentence on the subject appeared in parentheses, though it does not:

> The object of life, after all, is not to understand things, but to maintain one's defences and equilibrium and live as well as one can.

As they say, that one line was worth the price of the book.

Among the instruments of equilibrium Empson names (most are lexical, rather than strictly grammatical) there appears the coordinate conjunction "and." I had not perceived in such a common verbal waif such high calling. There's no question of it, though. Take these lines in Genesis:

> And Abel was a keeper of sheep, but Cain was a tiller of the ground. And in process of time it came to pass, that Cain brought of the fruit of the ground an offering unto the Lord. And Abel, he also brought of the firstlings of his flock and of the fat thereof. And the Lord had respect unto Abel and to his offering; but unto Cain and to his offering He had not respect. And Cain was very wroth and his countenance fell. And the Lord said unto Cain: "Why art thou wroth? and why is thy countenance

fallen? If thou doest well, shall it not be lifted up? and if thou doest not well, sin coucheth at the door; and unto thee is its desire, but thou mayest rule over it." And Cain spoke unto Abel his brother. And it came to pass, when they were in the field, that Cain rose up against Abel his brother, and slew him.

Was God

setting Cain up?

being honest?

wanting to encourage the younger of the two brothers—but being oblivious to the older's feelings?

all of the above?

Without cues like "so" or "because," we may surmise but can't finally establish the causative links between events in this passage. That short, mum's-the-word conjunction "and," all too simple in itself, complicates our understanding of the story.

My own favorite "and" appears in a quip attributed to Bertrand Russell. Asked to paraphrase George Santayana's rich but elusive theology, Russell is supposed to have said, "There is no God, and Mary is his mother." Other ambiguous "ands" that I have come across lately include Nicholas Kilmer's "furious, and wild, and peaceful" (about a country scene that he was painting) and a colleague's "frightening and sad and exhilarating" (about the prospect of changing careers).

In its small way, "and" can help us to keep life's sundry, necessary balls all up in the air at once. Nick Carraway, F. Scott Fitzgerald's narrator in *The Great Gatsby*, asserts, "Life is much more successfully looked at from a single window," but Fitzgerald himself once said, "The test of a first-rate intelligence is the ability to hold two opposing ideas in the mind at the same time and still retain the ability to function." Whether or not "first-rate intelligence" is the best name for the quality that he refers to, the need to see and live in poise with ambiguity is hard to deny in a world where much of humankind is stamped with Mona Lisa's (and Gatsby's and God's) inscrutability and physicists report that light is neither just particles nor just waves, but somehow both at once.

Coda

Grammar, then, can serve both our basic and our highest needs, when it's handled mindfully. Thinking, in my fifties, that perhaps I have arrived at a point for taking stock, I have used this book partly as an excuse for setting down what I now see those different needs to be. If, in conducting that inventory or advancing the linguistic practices described here, I have managed to provide my readers something of value, I am grateful.

One or two more paragraphs and I'll be gone.

Perhaps the world's best known grammatical joke is the one with which vaudevillians George Burns and Gracie Allen closed every episode of their television show in the 1950s. George would say,

Say "Good night," Gracie.

and scatterbrained Gracie, misunderstanding where the quotation marks fell in George's request, would compliantly and sweetly respond,

"Good night, Gracie."

It therefore seems appropriate that Gracie's last act of love toward George, who was her husband for thirty-eight years, should also involve grammatical wit. Rumor has it that she left a note for him to find after she died, a plea to him to go on living: "Never place a period where God has placed a comma."

We are neither done living nor done learning.

Acknowledgments

Not long ago, I had a dream in which our dinner guests were putting on their coats, readying to say good-bye and leave, when my wife, Diane, came running from the kitchen holding an oversized pot by two handles. In a voice of deep lament, she informed me, "You forgot to serve the alphabet soup!" I immediately sensed the enormity of my omission and somehow got a few of the guests to reseat themselves. Those few guests marveled at the letters and marks of punctuation floating in their bowls and spoons, and when they'd had their fills, they pronounced the soup "much better for a person than other kinds of food." By "better," they said, they meant both "more wholesome" and "more enlightening."

As soon as I woke from this dream, I knew it was really about the book in your hands. The surreal events reflected both my hesitation about going public with such a novel set of thoughts as this book and my hope that, if I did go public with it, it would prove worth the effort.

Truth to tell, I've had a slew of chefs in the kitchen with me. I owe them a great deal for whatever wholesomeness and tastiness this book has.

First and foremost is the woman in my dream with the big pot, who has figured in innumerable dreams of mine since 1970. Not only has she played the same role of booster in my waking world that she played during REM sleep, she is, in a real sense, co-creator of the book. She read and commented wisely on every draft (occasionally giving me the very words I was looking for), synthesized the many comments of other readers, tracked down sources for me, brainstormed with me for a title, compiled the book's index. . . . There is no aspect of this book untouched by her loving influence.

The other contributors to this book are numerous. They include (I say "include" on the strong hunch I am forgetting someone) all of the following good friends, students, and colleagues: Yusef Abdolmohammadi, Nicole Belmonte, Chris Beneke, Joan Bolker, Janet Buchwald, John Case, Sophia Chan, Angelique Davi, Karen Delorey, George Ellenbogen, Greg Farber, Evelyn Farbman, De Ann Finkel, Wayne Goins, Justin Hoskins, Paul Hughes, Martha Keating, Diane Kellogg, Christine Kraft, Rabbi Lawrence Kushner, Ray Mosher, Rob Ross, Nick Schupbach, Lynn Senne, Bob Sprich, and Judith Taplitz. I'm not sure that any author has been more blessed with the readers he needed both to prod him and to applaud him until the job was done.

In addition, I would like to single out six individuals whose comments on my drafts were unusually extensive: Richard Griffin, Jim Hornfischer, Nick Kilmer, my two children, Noam and Rachel Weinstein, and my brother, Warren Weinstein. (Warren's long, thoughtful commentary almost represents a book in its own right.) Their impact on the final text has been immense. Last but hardly least are the people at Quest Books. Time and again, my editor, Carolyn Bond, and the good-humored, very clear-eyed publishing manager at Quest, Sharron Dorr, simply refused to settle for language that would serve the needs of some readers but not most. First to last, they were your advocates, and if this book is readable, they deserve much of the credit.

My sincerest thanks to all.

Sources

Page vii. *"To know how near. . . ."* Nachman of Bratzlav, *Garden of the Souls: Rebbe Nachman on Suffering*, ed. Avraham Greenbaum (Monsey, NY: Breslov Research Institute, 1990). Quotation from p. 40.

INTRODUCTION

Page 1. *"The limits of my language. . . ."* Ludwig Wittgenstein, *Tractatus Logico-Philosophicus* (New York: Humanities Press, 1971). Quotation from p. 115 (section 5.6).

Page 2. *I did not begin.* Benjamin Lee Whorf, *Language, Thought, and Reality*, ed. John B. Carroll (Cambridge, MA: MIT Press, 1956). See pp. 221, 269.

Page 5. *"An only life. . . ."* Philip Larkin, *Collected Poems*, ed. Anthony Thwaite (London: Farrar, Straus, Giroux and the Marvell Press, 1989). Quotation from p. 208.

BOOTSTRAP GRAMMAR—TAKING LIFE IN HAND

Page 8. *At the far end.* Martin E. P. Seligman, *Helplessness— On Depression, Development, and Death* (San Francisco: W. H. Freeman, 1975). See pp. 184–88; Ellen J. Langer, *The*

Psychology of Control (Beverly Hills, CA: Sage Publications, 1983). See p. 101.

Getting Noticed

Page 9. "*If I am not. . . .*" Rabbi Hillel, *Pirkei Avot 1:14* (a tractate of the Mishna composed of ethical maxims of the Rabbis of the Mishnaic period).

Page 10. "*a lot less attractive. . . .*" Lewis Thomas, *The Medusa and the Snail: More Notes of a Biology Watcher* (New York: Viking Press, 1979). Quotation from p. 104.

Page 10. "*Sentences violating Rule 7. . . .*" William Strunk, Jr. and E. B. White, *The Elements of Style*, 2nd ed. (New York: Macmillan, 1972). Quotations from pp. 9, 2, and xii.

Energy

Page 15. "*any peace officer observing. . . .*" Lisa Grunwald and Stephen J. Adler, eds., *Letters of the Century* (New York: Dial Press, 1999). Quotation from p. 422.

Page 17. "*serves as a cop-out. . . .*" Albert Ellis and Robert Harper, *A New Guide to Rational Living* (Englewood Cliffs, NJ: Prentice-Hall, 1975). Quotation from p. xiv.

Doing What Works

Page 22. "*White men and women. . . .*" John Dawkins "Teaching Punctuation as a Rhetorical Tool." *College Composition and Communication*, 46.4 (December 1995): pp. 533–48. Alice Walker quoted on p. 539.

Page 22 "*In saying 'The tumult. . . .*" Margaret Bryant and Janet Rankin Aiken, *The Psychology of English* (New York: Columbia University Press, 1940). Quotation from p. 70.

GRAMMAR FOR CREATIVE PASSIVITY

Page 30. "*The right shot.* . . ." Eugen Herrigel, *Zen in the Art of Archery* (New York: Vintage Books, 1989). Quotation from pp. 50–51.

Page 31. "*because most deals fall.* . . ." Donald Trump, *Trump: The Art of the Deal* (New York: Random House, 1987). Quotation from p. 35.

Getting Out of One's Own Way

Page 32. "*Suppose that you kill.* . . ." William James, *Talks to Teachers on Psychology: And to Students on Some of Life's Ideals* (New York: Henry Holt, 1925). Quotation from p. 152.

Page 32. "*Use the active voice.* . . ." William Strunk, Jr. and E. B. White, *Elements of Style*, 2nd ed. (New York: Macmillan, 1972). Quotation from p. 13.

Page 33. *By contrast, the grammarian.* Otto Jespersen, *The Philosophy of Grammar.* (New York: W. W. Norton, 1924). See pp. 167–68.

Page 35. "*the moment.* . . ." Morton Eustis, *Players at Work* (New York: Theatre Arts, 1937). Quotation from p. 18.

The Latent Repertoire

Page 36. "*All clearings promise.*" Philip Booth, "How to See Deer," in *Lifelines: Selected Poems 1950–1999* (New York: Viking, 1999). Quotation from p. 77.

Page 38. "*We are endeavoring.* . . ." Edward T. Thompson, *Reader's Digest: How to Write Clearly*, www.harmonize.com/PROBE/Aids/manual/Write_cl.htm.

Hybrid

Page 40. "*Teach us to care....*" T. S. Eliot, "Ash Wednesday," *The Complete Poems and Plays* (New York: Harcourt, Brace and World, 1971). Quotation from p. 67.

Page 42. "*make direct amends....*" 12 Steps of Alcoholics Anonymous, quotations from: http://www.alcoholicsanony mous.org/en_information_aa.cfm?PageID=17&SubPage=68.

GRAMMAR FOR BELONGING

Page 44. "*If I am not....*" Rabbi Hillel. See note for pg. 9.

Touch

Page 47. "*warm, imaginative touch....*" John Trimble, *Writing with Style: Conversations on the Art of Writing* (Englewood Cliffs, NJ: Prentice-Hall, 1975). Quotation from p. 19.

Page 47. "*Someone walks in....*" Walker Gibson, *The "Speaking Voice" and the Teaching of Composition* (New York: College Entrance Examination Board, 1965). Quotation from p. 6.

Page 49. "*Gentlemen: Here I am....*" Lisa Grunwald and Stephen J. Adler, eds., *Letters of the Century* (New York: Dial Press, 1999). Quotation from p. 571.

Page 49. "*Punctuation—just one of....*" John Dawkins, "Teaching Punctuation as a Rhetorical Tool," *College Composition and Communication*, 46, no. 4 (December 1995): pp. 533–48. Quotation from p. 533.

Communication

Page 52. "*One should not aim....*" Quintilian, *The Orator's Education*, book 8.2.

Page 56. Lynne Truss, *Eats, Shoots and Leaves: The Zero Tolerance Approach to Punctuation* (New York: Gotham Books, 2004).

Bonding

Page 59. "*[the person] who pays....*" e. e. cummings, *Collected Poems* (San Diego, CA: Harcourt, Brace, 1938). Quotation from p. 180.

Page 60. "*This is Just....*" William Carlos Williams, *Selected Poems* (New York: New Directions, 1968). Quotation from p. 55.

Being Correct

Page 64. "*A language is a....*" Max Weinreich, "Der YIVO un di problemen fun undzer tsayt," *YIVO Bletter* 25 no. 1 (January-February 1945): pp. 3–18. Quotation from p. 13.

Compromise

Page 65. "*acute, tuned up....*" John Barth, *The End of the Road* (New York: Bantam Books, 1969). Quotation from p. 134.

Page 68. "*When feasible, use plural....*" Maxine C. Hairston, *Successful Writing* (New York: W. W. Norton, 1981). Quotations from pp. 124–26.

Page 69. "*prefer geniality to....*" Henry Watson Fowler and Francis George Fowler, *The King's English* (Oxford, England: Clarendon Press, 1930). Quotation from p. 70.

Page 70. "*must modify itself if....*" Eric Partridge, *Usage and Abusage* (New York: Norton and Company, 1997). Quotation from p. 134.

Trust

Page 72. "*Look! they say. . . .*" Lewis Thomas, *The Medusa and the Snail: More Notes of a Biology Watcher* (New York: Viking Press, 1979). Quotation from pp. 104–5.

Generosity

Page 75. "*isn't ready. . . .*" John Trimble, *Writing with Style: Conversations on the Art of Writing* (Englewood Cliffs, NJ: Prentice-Hall, 1975). Quotation from p. 101.

Page 76. "*We try to do. . . .*" Samuel Butler, *The Notebooks of Samuel Butler*, ed. Francis Hackett and Henry Festing Jones (Boston: E. P. Dutton, 1917). Quotation from p. 94.

Page 76. "*I could not imagine. . . .*"Annie Dillard, *The Writing Life* (New York: Harper and Row, 1990). Quotations from pp. 99, 100, 105.

Page 77. "*It is almost always. . . .*" Lewis Thomas, *The Medusa and the Snail: More Notes of a Biology Watcher* (New York: Viking Press, 1979). Quotation from p. 104.

Page 78. "*modify the statement. . . .*" Francis Christensen, *Notes toward a New Rhetoric: Six Essays for Teachers* (New York: Harper and Row, 1978). Quotations from pp. 5, 12.

Friends in the Graveyard

Page 80. *Of all my comforters.* Michel de Montaigne, *The Autobiography of Michel de Montaigne*, ed. Marvin Lowenthal (Boston and New York: Houghton Mifflin, 1935). See p. 283. Quotations from pp. 80, 142.

Page 81. "*No activity can become. . . .*" Hannah Arendt, *The Portable Hannah Arendt*, ed. Peter R. Baehr (New York: Penguin Classics, 2003). Quotation from p. 199.

Page 82. Nilo Cruz, *Anna in the Tropics* (New York: Theatre Communications Group, 2003).

Page 82. Malcolm X and Alex Haley, *Autobiography of Malcolm X* (New York: Ballantine Books, 1992). Quotation from p. 173.

Page 82. *read in plain view.* Marcus Aurelius, *Meditations* (Chicago: Henry Regency Co., 1956). See p. xiii.

Page 82. *in the Hopi language.* Benjamin Lee Whorf, *Language, Thought, and Reality,* ed. John B. Carroll (Cambridge, MA: The MIT Press, 1956). See pp. 59–61, 139–40.

GRAMMAR FOR FREEDOM

Page 86. *"I have known...."* T. S. Eliot, "The Love Song of J. Alfred Prufrock," *The Complete Poems and Plays* (New York: Harcourt, Brace and World, Inc., 1971). Quotation from p. 5.

Modeling I-Statements

Page 89. *"You stop pestering...."* Thomas Gordon, *P.E.T.— Parent Effectiveness Training: The Tested New Way to Raise Responsible Children* (New York: New American Library, 1975). Quotation from p. 121.

Page 89. *A caveat.* Haim Ginott, *Between Parent and Child* (New York: Avon, 1965). Quotation from p. 59.

Using E-Prime

Page 91. *"The little word...."* George Santayana, *Scepticism and Animal Faith: Introduction to a System of Philosophy* (New York: Dover Publications, 1955). Quotation from p. 71.

Page 92. *"may be a very...."* Alfred Korzybski, *Science and*

Sanity: An Introduction to Non-Aristotelian Systems and General Semantics (Fort Worth, TX: Institute of General Semantics, 1958). Quotation from p. 758.

Page 92. David Bourland, Jr. *To Be or Not to Be: E-Prime as a Tool for Critical Thought* (Institute of General Semantics, http://www.esgs.org/uk/art/epr1.htm).

Page 93. "*when [people] say. . . .*" Albert Ellis and Robert Harper, *A New Guide to Rational Living* (Englewood Cliffs, NJ: Prentice-Hall, 1975). Quotation from p. xii.

Our Linguistic Limits

Page 100. "*Then the Lord God. . . .*" Genesis 2:7 in *The Holy Scriptures* (Philadelphia: Jewish Publication Society of America, 1917). Quotation from p. 4.

GRAMMAR TO RESTORE THE EGO

Fulcrum

Page 104. "*its own place. . . .*" John Milton, *Paradise Lost*, ed. Merritt Y. Hughes (Indianapolis: Bobbs-Merrill, 1962). Quotation from p. 13.

Grammar, Thing of Beauty

Page 105. "*Grammar is a piano. . . .*" Joan Didion, "Why I Write," in *Joan Didion: Essays and Conversations,* ed. Ellen G. Friedman (Princeton, NJ: Ontario Review Press, 1984). Quotation from p. 7.

Page 106. "*Not too long ago. . . .*" Barbara Ehrenreich, *The Worst Years of Our Lives* (New York: Pantheon Books, 1990). Quotation from p. 22.

Page 107. *"It does not seem. . . ."* Malcolm Gladwell, "Annals of Commerce: The Terrazzo Jungle," *The New Yorker* (March 15, 2004): pp. 120–27. Quotation from pp. 121–22.

Page 108. *"Miguel Maldonado is nineteen. . . ."* Richard Currey, *Crossing Over: The Vietnam Stories* (Livingston, MT: Clark City Press, 1993). Quotation from pp. 25–26.

Page 109. *"to take [one's] agony. . . ."* Joe McGinniss, *Heroes* (New York: Viking Press, 1976). Quotation from p. 121.

Page 109. *"We pull each. . . ."* James Frey, *A Million Little Pieces* (New York: Anchor Books, 2005). Quotation from pp. 307–8.

Page 109. *"The show was over. . . ."* Annie Dillard, *The Writing Life* (New York: Harper and Row, 1990). Quotations from pp. 97–98.

GRAMMAR FOR MINDFULNESS

Page 112. *"You shall no longer. . . ."* Walt Whitman, *Leaves of Grass* (New York: Modern Library, 1977). Quotation from p. 25.

Page 112. *"Existentialism means no one. . . ."* Delmore Schwartz, "Does Existentialism Still Exist?" *Partisan Review* (December 1948). Quotation from p. 1361.

Page 112. *"Hear, O Israel. . . ."* Deuteronomy 6:4.

Speaking Without Feigning Certainty: Part I

Page 115. *"We commonly do not. . . ."* Henry David Thoreau, *The Annotated Walden*, ed. Philip Van Doren

Stern (New York: Clarkson N. Potter, 1970). Quotation from p. 145.

Speaking Without Feigning Certainty: Part II

Page 118. "*Pain—has an Element. . . .*" Emily Dickinson, *The Complete Poems,* ed. Thomas H. Johnson (Boston: Little, Brown and Co., 1960). Quotation from p. 323.

Page 118. "*When a thought takes. . . .*" Emily Dickinson, *Selected Poems,* ed. Conrad Aiken (New York: Modern Library, 1948). Quotation from p. viii.

Page 119. "*Pain has an element. . . .*" Emily Dickinson, *Poems,* eds. Mabel Loomis Todd and T. W. Higginson (Boston: Little, Brown and Co., 1910). Quotation from p. 33.

Page 119. "*habit of handwriting.*" R. W. Franklin, *The Editing of Emily Dickinson: A Reconsideration* (Madison: University of Wisconsin Press, 1967). Quotation from p. 120.

A Digression on the Spiritual Value of Dictionaries

Page 127. "*There's a time. . . .*" Ecclesiastes 3:1.

Tolerating Ambiguity

Pages 129–130. "*second-type ambiguity.*" William Empson, *Seven Types of Ambiguity* (New York: New Directions Books, 1966). Quotations from table of contents and p. 247.

Page 130. "*And Abel was a. . . .*"Genesis 4:2–8.

Page 131. *My own favorite* and. Quotation from website: http://salon.blogspot.com/2002_08_01_salon_archive.html.

Page 131. "*furious, and wild. . . .*" Nicholas Kilmer, *A Place in*

Normandy (New York: Henry Holt and Co., 1997). Quotation from p. 243.

Page 132. "*Life is much more....*" F. Scott Fitzgerald, *The Great Gatsby* (New York: Charles Scribner's Sons, 1925). Quotation from p. 4.

Page 132. "*The test of a....*" F. Scott Fitzgerald, *The Crack-up,* ed. Edmund Wilson (New York: New Directions Books, 1945). Quotation on p. 69.

Coda

Page 134. "*Never place a period....*" Used in the "God Is Still Speaking" campaign of the United Church of Christ.

Index

active verb, 4
active voice, 13–18, 32–34, 41–42
adverb, 18, 19, 51
adverbial intensifiers, 3
adverbial qualifiers, 123–24
affection, 44, 60. *See also* love
agency, 8, 14–16, 18–19, 22, 24, 30–31, 33, 40, 42, 45, 67, 129. *See also* autonomy
Aiken, Janet Rankin, 22
Alcoholics Anonymous, 42
Algonquin Indians, 54n
Allen, Gracie, 133
ambiguity, 129–32
Amidah, 100
"and," 24, 91, 129–32
Anna in the Tropics (Cruz), 82
Anna Karenina, 82
apostrophe, 4, 61–62
appositive, 106
Arendt, Hannah, 81
Aristotle, 11, 63
Armstrong, Neil, 83
"Ash Wednesday" (Eliot), 40
assertiveness, 11, 12
attentiveness, attention, 12,

61, 90, 114. *See also* mindfulness
"Aubade" (Larkin), 5
Aurelius, Marcus, 82
authority, challenge to authority, 24, 66
autonomy, 30. *See also* agency
Awa, Kenzo, 30

balance, imbalance, 4, 11, 40, 42. *See also* equilibrium
Barth, John, 65–66
Beatles, The, 98
beauty, 105–6, 109, 110
belonging, 43, 45
Bible, 112. *See also* Ecclesiastes, Genesis, Hebrew
Black English, 63
blessing, 40–42
bonding, 57–58. *See also* community
Booth, Philip, 36
Bourland Jr., D. David, 92
Bruce, Lenny, 15
Bryant, Margaret M., 22
Burns, George, 133
"but," 4, 24, 103–4

Butler, Samuel, 76

Cain and Abel, 130–31
Camus, Albert, 82
Captain Ahab, 83
Carraway, Nick, 132
certainty, uncertainty, 4, 42, 114, 115, 117. *See also* confusion, disclaimer, fallibility
Chinese, China, 2, 82, 103
Christensen, Francis, 78–79
Churchill, Winston, 121
Cockney, 63
Cohen, Leonard, 120
colon, 8–12, 112
comma, 5, 20–23, 49, 56, 75, 118, 134
communication, 1, 22, 52, 61, 62
community, 51, 57, 63, 72, 82, 86–87, 103, 129. *See also* bonding
companionship, company, 46, 50
compromise, 65, 69–70
confusion, 23, 53. *See also* certainty
conjunction, 4, 24, 103, 130–31. *See also* "and," "but"
consciousness, 17, 124
contraction, 66
Cruz, Nilo, 82
"Cult of Busyness" (Ehrenreich), 106

cummings, e. e., 59
cumulative sentence, 75, 77–78
Currey, Richard, 107–9

dash (punctuation), 3, 4, 118–20
Dawkins, John, 49–50
Death Row, 122–23
decisiveness, 4
depression, 8, 15
dialect, 63
Diary of a Writer (Dostoyevsky), 48n
Dickinson, Emily, 118–20
dictionary, 125–28. *See also* Webster's
Didion, Joan, 105
Dillard, Annie, 76, 109–10
disclaimer, 119, 120. *See also* certainty
Dostoyevsky, Fyodor, 48n
double negative, 55
dust, 1, 100

Eats, Shoots and Leaves (Truss), 56n
Ecclesiastes, 127
Ehrenreich, Barbara, 106
Elements of Style, The (Strunk and White), 10, 32
Eliot, T. S., 40, 86
ellipsis, 4, 57–59
Ellis, Albert, 17, 93
empowerment, 16, 19
Empson, William, 129–30

End of the Road, The
  (Barth), 65–66
E-Prime, 91–94, 95, 99
equilibrium, 130. *See also*
  balance
ethos, 63
exclamation mark, 26, 49,
  71–72
expansiveness, 3, 37, 75, 77.
  See also generosity

failure, 52, 102. *See also*
  setback
fallibility, 116. *See also*
  certainty
fear, 2, 87. *See also* trauma
first-person pronoun, 4, 45,
  90, 115. *See also* "I"
Fitzgerald, F. Scott, 132
Fowler, H. W. and Francis G.,
  69
fragments, 2, 23, 47, 54. *See
  also* sentence fragment
Franklin, R. W., 119
freedom, 85, 98
free will, 8
Freud, Sigmund, 44
Frey, James, 109
Frost, Robert, 119n
future tense, 4, 121

generosity, 4, 75, 78, 79. *See
  also* expansiveness
Genesis, 100, 130
Gibson, Walker, 47–48
Giuliani, Rudy, 121

Gladwell, Malcolm, 107
"glamour" (etymology), 105
God, 100, 112, 131–32, 134
Gordon, Thomas, 89
grammatical profile, 3
Great Gatsby, The
  (Fitzgerald), 132
Gruen, Victor, 107
Guiding Light, The, 48–49
Guofan, General Zeng, 103

Hairston, Maxine, 68
Hamlet (Shakespeare), 99n
Harper, Robert A., 17, 93
Hayes, Helen, 35
Hebrew, 100, 112
Hendrix, Jimi, 110
Herrigel, Eugen, 30
Higginson, Thomas
  Wentworth, 118
Hillel, Rabbi, 9, 44
hopefulness, hopelessness,
  hope, 4, 8, 41, 45, 121
Hopi Indians, 2, 82
Hurt, Mississippi John, 57,
  60

"I," 9, 32–33, 44, 115–16.
  See also first-person
  pronoun
imbalance. See *balance*
imperative, 25–27
instrumentality, 19
intensifier, 3, 71
intimacy, 47, 57, 59
intransitive verb, 14, 17

I-statement, 88–89, 99
italics, 3, 71, 73, 129

James, William, 32
Jespersen, Otto, 33

Kali (Hindu goddess), 42
Kellogg III, E. W., 93
kidney stone, 80
Kilmer, Nicholas, 131
kinesics, 48
Kipling, Rudyard, 22
Korzybski, Count Alfred, 91–92

Laing, R. D., 87
Langer, Ellen, 8
Larkin, Philip, 5
Latin, 55
Lear, King, 120
linguistic Everyman, 53
love, 56, 59, 125–26. See also affection
"Love Song of J. Alfred Prufrock, The" (Eliot), 86

Malcolm X, 82
Maldonado, Miguel, 108
Manutius, Aldus, 48
"may" (subjunctive), 41
meekness, 12
Melville, Herman, 83
Michelangelo, 35
Miller, Arthur, 109
Milton, John, 104
mindfulness, 111, 113–14, 116, 120. See also attentiveness
misplaced modifier, 53
Mona Lisa, 132
Monet, Claude, 58–59
Montaigne, 80–81

Nachman of Bratzlav, vii
name(s), 44, 98–100
narrative therapy, 104
New Guide to Rational Living, A (Ellis and Harper), 93
nonsexist alternatives, 67–68

obsession, 126, 128. See also preoccupation
"Ode to the West Wind" (Shelley), 81
Ortiz, David, 40, 42

Parent Effectiveness Training in Action (Gordon), 89
parenthesis, 3, 47, 130
Partridge, Eric, 70
passive verb, 4, 14, 94
passive voice, 14–15, 31–35, 41–42
passivity (creative), 29–42, 129
past imperfect tense, 96
past perfect tense, 96
past tense, 95–96, 99
period (punctuation), 4, 77, 118, 134
periodic sentence, 78

P. E. T. *See* Parent Effectiveness Training
Pope, Alexander, 83
positive self-regard, 102. *See also* self-esteem
possessive, 62
preoccupation, 114, 121, 126, 128. *See also* obsession
preposition, 18–19, 38
present imperfect tense, 96
present ongoing (tense), 95
present tense, 80, 83, 84, 95, 96, 107
private language, 3
pronoun, 54n, 65, 67–69, 91, 115. *See also* nonsexist alternatives
pronoun reference, 53
proper noun, 98
Psychology of English (Bryant and Aiken), 22

question mark, 3
Quintilian, 52
quotation mark, 48, 53, 84, 133

Rand, Ayn, 127
"Rape of the Lock" (Pope), 83
receptivity, 30
repetition, 105, 107
respect, 11, 25, 63
responsibility, responsiveness, 14, 16, 40, 72, 74
risk-taking, 21
Rolling Stones, 98

Roosevelt, Franklin Delano, 38
rule-rigidity, 20
Russell, Bertrand, 131

Sanskrit, 42
Santayana, George, 91, 131
Schwartz, Delmore, 112
Science and Sanity (Korzybski), 91
Scottish, 105n
self-esteem, 4. *See also* positive regard
Seligman, Martin, 8
semicolon, 10, 75–77
sentence fragment, 23, 54. *See also* fragment
setback, 4, 73, 103. *See also* failure
Seven Types of Ambiguity (Empson), 129
sexist language, 67–68. *See also* nonsexist alternatives
Shakespeare, William, 99n
Shelley, Percy, 81
Shema, 112
Skinner, B. F., 38
Spanglish, 63
speech inflection, 11
"Star Spangled Banner," 110
Stevens, Wallace, 21–22
stroking, 46–47, 73. *See also* touch
Strunk, William, 10, 32
subjunctive verb, 41
subordinate clause, 104

Tacitus, 81

tennis, 30

tense shift, 2, 55

third-person omniscient, 115–16

third-person pronoun, 67, 69

"This Is Just to Say" (Williams), 59–60

Thomas, Lewis, 10, 11, 72, 77

Thoreau, Henry David, 8, 115

"to be" (forms of the verb), 4, 91–93, 95

Todd, Mabel Loomis, 118

touch, 20, 46, 73. *See also* stroking

transactional psychologist, 46

transitive verb, 13–17

trauma, 2, 20, 75

Trimble, John, 47, 75

triple-spacing, 36–38

Trump, Donald, 31

Truss, Lynne, 56n

trust, 4, 71–72

uncertainty. *See* certainty

ungenerosity. *See* generosity

Vietnam, 107

(Virgin) Mary, 131

voice, 26, 47–50, 61

Voltaire, 71–72

Vygotsky, Lev, 48n

Walden (Thoreau), 115

Walker, Alice, 22

"we"(plural pronoun), 45

Webster's Seventh New Collegiate Dictionary, 125–28

Weinreich, Max, 64

Weinstein, Warren, 80

White, E. B., 10, 32

Whitman, Walt, 79, 112

Whorf, Benjamin Lee, 2–3, 82

"will" (auxiliary verb), 121–22

Williams, William Carlos, 59–60

Wittgenstein, Ludwig, 1

Writing with Style (Trimble), 47, 75

"you" (second-person pronoun), 88–89, 91

Zen in the Art of Archery (Herrigel), 30

Zuo, General, 103

QUEST BOOKS

encourages open-minded inquiry into
world religions, philosophy, science, and the arts
in order to understand the wisdom of the ages,
respect the unity of all life, and help people explore
individual spiritual self-transformation.

Its publications are generously supported by
THE KERN FOUNDATION,
a trust committed to Theosophical education.

Quest Books is the imprint of
the Theosophical Publishing House,
a division of the Theosophical Society in America.
For information about programs, literature,
on-line study, membership benefits, and international centers,
see **www.theosophical.org**
or call 800-669-1571 or (outside the U.S.) 630-668-1571.

To order books or a complete Quest catalog,
call 800-669-9425 or (outside the U.S.) 630-665-0130.